Contents

Foreword by Allan Massie

1 Planning and preparation
- Best time of year and weather — 6
- How long will it take? — 6
- Terrain and gradients — 8
- Waymarking and navigation — 9
- Getting there and away — 10
- Facilities along the Way — 11
- Access issues and dogs — 12
- Cycling — 13
- Common Ridings — 13
- What to bring — 13
- Packing checklist — 14

2 Background
- 2·1 History — 15
- 2·2 Geology and scenery — 18
- 2·3 Habitats and wildlife — 20

3 Route description
- Tweedbank to Melrose — 27
- Melrose and Melrose Abbey — 28
- 3·1 Melrose to Kelso — 29
- Dryburgh Abbey — 34
- 3·2 Kelso to Jedburgh — 38
- Kelso — 38
- Kelso Abbey — 39
- 3·3 Jedburgh to Hawick — 45
- Jedburgh — 45
- Jedburgh Abbey — 46
- 3·4 Hawick to Selkirk — 53
- Hawick — 53
- 3·5 Selkirk to Melrose — 62
- Selkirk — 62
- Abbotsford House — 66

4 Reference
- Contact details, travel and accommodation — 68
- SOAC, further reading, maps and credits — 69
- Index — 70

Foreword

I would like to have had this book years ago, when I would have been able to make practical use of it to walk the Borders Abbeys Way. It is aimed primarily at walkers, and gives them necessary and detailed information, and good advice as to what they should do and what they would be wise to avoid. But it offers more than that. It is also a guide to the social and cultural history of the Borderland, to the past as well as the present.

The four ruined abbeys – Melrose, Dryburgh, Kelso and Jedburgh – are at the heart of the route. But it goes further, inviting you to Hawick where there has never been an abbey, and to Selkirk where the abbey survived for only a few years in the 12th century before the monks decamped to Kelso, with its richer pastureland for their sheep. Indeed it offers an outline history of the Borders from the generally peaceful and prosperous reign of King David I, the founder of the abbeys, through the ravages of English invasions, the rough reiving centuries, and the flourishing of the Borders in the 18th century Enlightenment.

In short, it's a book to be read for pleasure as well as use. Even those of us who think we know the Borders may be reminded of things we had forgotten – in my case The Temple of the Muses commemorating the poet James Thomson. Newcomers to the Borders will find this book a splendid introduction to its history, legends and wildlife.

Allan Massie, author and journalist

Borders Abbeys Way

Neil Mackay

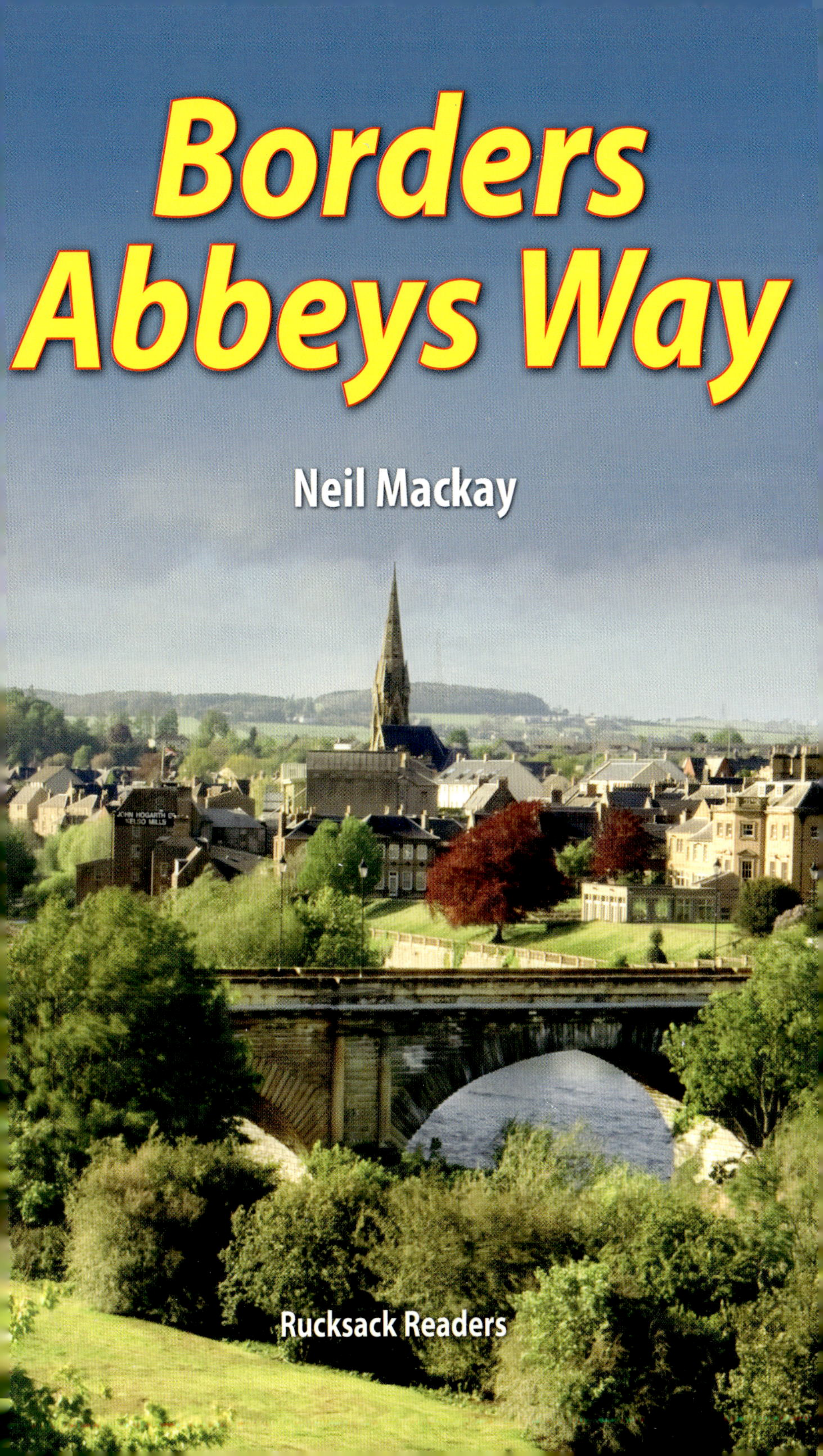

Rucksack Readers

Borders Abbeys Way

Published in 2017 by Rucksack Readers,
6 Old Church Lane, Edinburgh, EH15 3PX, UK
telephone +44/0 131 661 0262
website *www.rucsacs.com*
email info@rucsacs.com

Distributed in North America by Interlink Publishing, 46 Crosby Street, Northampton, Mass., 01060, USA (*www.interlinkbooks.com*)

Text, design and mapping © Rucksack Readers; photographs © Rucksack Readers and licensors: see page 69 for credits.

The rights of Neil Mackay to be identified as the author of this work have been asserted by him in accordance with the Copyright, Designs and Patents Act 1988.

All rights reserved. No part of this publication may be reproduced, transmitted or stored in a retrieval system, in any form or by any means, without prior permission in writing from Rucksack Readers.

ISBN 978-1-898481-78-2

British Library cataloguing in publication data: a catalogue record for this book is available from the British Library.

Designed in Scotland by Ian Clydesdale (*www.workhorse.co.uk*).

Printed and bound in Poland by Pario Print, Kraków: *www.parioprint.pl*

Publisher's note

All information was checked carefully prior to publication. However, new services start up, rural businesses open and close, and routes evolve. Along the route, look out for waymarkers and follow any local diversions. Prior to departure, please check the websites listed at the top of page 68.

The weather in Scotland is unpredictable year-round, and parts of the Way are exposed and remote from sources of help. Do not rely on having reception on a mobile phone. You are responsible for your own safety, and for ensuring that your clothing, food and equipment are suited to your needs. The publisher cannot accept any liability for any ill-health, accident or loss arising directly or indirectly from reading this book.

Feedback is welcome and will be rewarded

We welcome comments and suggestions: please email us at **info@rucsacs.com**. All feedback will be followed up, and if comments lead to changes, readers will be entitled to claim a free copy of our next edition upon publication.

1 Planning and preparation

The Borders Abbeys Way is a very pleasing walk for experienced walkers and beginners alike. It is an easygoing circuit of 67 miles (108 km), often started and finished in the pretty market town of Melrose, one of the most visited and accessible towns of the Borders. Melrose is only about 40 miles (65 km) south of Edinburgh, reached easily by train, bus or car. The route has modest ascents and descents, and is waymarked clearly and consistently. The Way was developed by Scottish Borders Council, which also maintains it, and the route was completed in 2006. It has been recognised as one of Scotland's Great Trails.

Named after the famous 12th century abbeys that the Way visits, your walk circumnavigates the central Borders using ancient drove roads and paths, through an area of picturesque scenery, diverse wildlife, unique history and welcoming hospitality.

The Way is a circuit, more oval than circular. It can be started at any of the five main towns – Melrose, Kelso, Jedburgh, Hawick or Selkirk. It can be completed in five days with an overnight stopover at each, or six days if (as recommended) you split the long Melrose/Kelso section into two with an overnight in St Boswells.

Part 3 provides a detailed route description for following the Way clockwise, the direction generally agreed to provide the best views. Although we start and finish at Melrose, you can follow our sections in any order. If you live within striking range, you may wish to complete the Way in a couple of long weekends or even day walks, using local buses to return to your starting points.

River Teviot near Nisbet

Best time of year and weather

Fortunately for those who have little choice over their holiday dates, any time of year can be suitable, although winter months have predictable disadvantages. Scotland can have cold wet weather at any time of the year, or, if you are lucky, crisp dry days filled with sunshine. Think about the following before making plans:

 Winter walking is less flexible: at this latitude, the days are short, in late December as few as 6-7 hours of daylight as opposed to 16-18 hours in late June.

 Weather at any time of the year can be changeable: see page 69 for sources of weather forecasts.

 Public transport in winter months can be less frequent, therefore plan your walk accordingly. Local transport operator websites are on page 68.

 Many visitor attractions are closed out of season (typically October to April).

 Summer months may bring pests such as midges (small biting insects) and/or clegs (horse-flies), although usually only in still weather.

 Accommodation in summer months can be under pressure when visitor numbers are high; in winter some B&Bs close.

Ideally if you can choose your holiday dates, the optimum months are likely to be May/June and early September/October. Also bear in mind the Borders Common Riding festivals dates: see page 13. Peak summer months are July/August, with demand high for accommodation. Always book accommodation well in advance.

How long will it take?

The Way can be completed by fast walkers in five days, at the price of a very long first day and no time to make side-trips. For most people it makes more sense to allow six walking days. How you complete the Way depends not only on your fitness and attitude, but also on your time constraints and the pace you find comfortable. Don't underestimate the time you need to appreciate fine scenery and look out for wildlife.

Towards the Minto hills

Allow time to explore the towns *en route* and especially the abbeys, which generally open at 9.30 or 10.00 depending on the season. Each abbey visit needs about an hour, and in some you will want to linger longer, e.g. to climb to the roof or visit a museum. The table opposite shows the daily distances for two itineraries.

If the first day's distance of 17·9 miles (28·8 km) feels too long, you can shorten your first day's walk from Melrose, stopping to take a leisurely visit at Dryburgh Abbey 4 miles (6·4 km) from Melrose, and going slightly off-route to overnight at nearby St Boswells. If you then retrace your steps to Dryburgh, the next day's walk would be 15 miles/24·2 km to Kelso, but if you stay south of the Tweed on St Cuthbert's Way, you can rejoin the Borders Abbeys Way after only 2 miles/3 km at Mertoun Bridge, shortening the second day's distance to 13·7 mi/22·1 km.

Other options include the Eildon Hill North route out of Melrose. This adds only 0·6 miles (1 km) to your journey, but it includes a stiff climb to 404 m/1325 ft, which allows you to enjoy superb views from the Eildons. It combines well with a detour to Dryburgh Abbey and overnight in St Boswells on our six-day itinerary. Finally, if you take the drove road option out of Hawick, you will add 2·1 miles (3·4 km) to your day's walk.

If completing the Way as a single expedition seems too challenging, splitting the circuit into shorter sections is a further option. There are many ways to divide it into manageable sections, using public transport to return to your starting point.

Distances

	Five-day walk			Six-day walk		
	miles	km		miles	km	pages
Melrose			Melrose			
				4·7	7·6	29-33
	17·9	28·8	St Boswells			
				15·0	24·2	33-37
Kelso			Kelso			
	13·0	20·9		13·0	20·9	38-44
Jedburgh			Jedburgh			
	13·2	21·3		13·2	21·3	45-52
Hawick			Hawick			
	12·8	20·6		12·8	20·6	53-61
Selkirk			Selkirk			
	10·5	16·9		10·5	16·9	62-67
Melrose			Melrose			
Total	**67·4**	**108·5**	**Total**	**69·2**	**111·5**	

Terrain and gradients

The Way is fairly well used, and paths across even grassy ground may be well-trampled. The terrain is mixed, ranging from minor roads, good tracks on farm and forest roads, to field and riverside paths which may have muddy or boggy sections, depending on recent weather conditions. Where there are streams to cross, timber footbridges are provided. Access through fences and walls is generally by gate, although there are occasional stiles to climb.

There are hillside sections where lighter use makes the paths less obvious, but waymarkers provide reassurance. These stretches can feel exposed and remote, and must be taken seriously, especially when weather conditions are poor and visibility is compromised. Always check the weather forecast before setting out: sources are listed on page 69.

The Way generally features many minor rises and falls through gentle rolling countryside, and the main Way never goes above 338 m (1110 ft) above sea level. There are also some notable climbs, and in order to complete the whole route you will gain a total of 1625 m (5330 ft) of altitude.

The altitude profile on the inside back cover shows ascents and descents along the Way, assuming you start from Melrose and stick to the main Way. Studying the profile can help you to plan your preferred itinerary.

Waymarking and navigation

The Way is waymarked clearly and consistently along its entire length with distinctive Borders Abbeys Way waymarkers, either on timber posts or attached to walls or lamp-posts. At major junctions, timber fingerposts with inscribed lettering are often prominent from a distance. Other than in low cloud or thick mist, waymarkers are generally intervisible even across high ground. However, remember that waymarkers can occasionally become overgrown with vegetation or damaged by animals or people.

If you have never tackled a long-distance walk before, the Way is a good first choice; you may benefit from reading our *Notes for novices*: see page 69. Inexperienced walkers may find it more enjoyable, as well as safer, to have company, ideally someone who can read a map and compass. However, it is generally when you make decisions for yourself that you learn to navigate.

The Eildon Hill North alternative from Melrose is waymarked as the St Cuthbert Way/ Eildon Hill Walk as far as the saddle of the Eildon Hills, thereafter follow our directions carefully to Eildon Mains. The alternative Waverley Walk approach into Hawick is not waymarked, but follows a well-surfaced route. The drove road option out of Hawick is not waymarked at first, and some of its waymarks (white horseshoe on blue) are very faded. Again, follow our directions closely until you rejoin the Borders Abbeys Way.

On minor and single-track roads stay alert for other road users. If there are no pavements or verges, walk on the right side of the road so as to face oncoming traffic. The only exception is where poor sight lines temporarily make it safer to use the left side. Drivers may not be expecting to see walkers: help them by wearing bright colours, especially when visibility is poor.

The mapping in this book is all you need to follow the Way, although it's advisable to read about the route ahead in advance. Study the route description and maps for an idea of where you *should* be going. Carrying a compass is also sensible, provided that you know how to use it. Smart mobile phones have an accurate compass and many walking and mapping apps are available. For more about maps, printed and online, see page 69.

Getting there and away

For anybody who prefers trains, the easiest access to the Way is the Borders Railway from Edinburgh to Tweedbank station (re-opened in 2015). The link from Tweedbank to Melrose can be completed by bus or on foot, see page 27. For rail travel from the south, an alternative to coming via Edinburgh would be to take a 67 bus from Berwick railway station to Kelso or Melrose.

Bus services are provided by several operators, many running express buses as well as local. In 2017 Borders Buses took over First Scotland East, and route numbers shown below may change in future: for updated timetables and services, see www.bustimes.org.uk or www.travelinescotland.com. Some further transport websites are listed on page 68.

Borders Buses operate the X62 between Edinburgh and Melrose via Peebles; the X95 between Edinburgh and Carlisle via Galashiels, Selkirk and Hawick; and the 72 bus between Melrose and Selkirk (Mondays to Fridays): see www.bordersbuses.co.uk.

Peter Hogg (of Jedburgh) runs the useful number 20 route between Jedburgh and Hawick via Denholm: see www.roadhoggs.net.

Perryman's Buses operates routes 51 (Jedburgh to Edinburgh) and 52 (Kelso to Edinburgh) via St Boswells. They also run the 67 between Galashiels and Berwick railway station via Tweedbank, Melrose, St Boswells and Kelso. And there's a 68 between Galashiels and Jedburgh, via Tweedbank, Melrose and St Boswells: see www.perrymansbuses.co.uk.

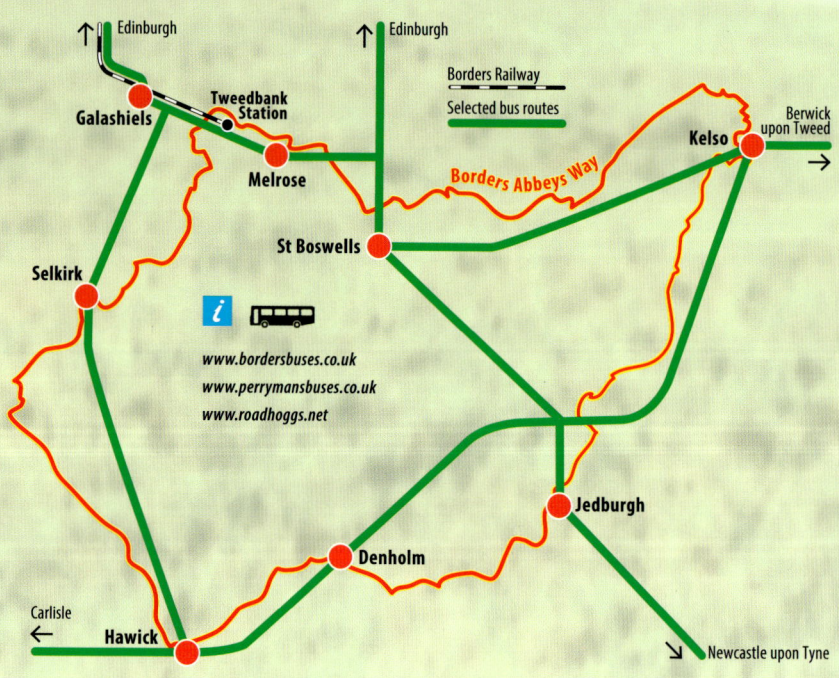

Facilities along the Way

	distances off the Way						
	miles	km	map page	B&B/hotel	campsite	pub/café	food shop
Melrose			30	✓	✓	✓	✓
Newton St Boswells			32			✓	✓
St Boswells	0·8	1·4	32	✓		✓	✓
Kelso			37	✓		✓	✓
Harestanes VC	1·6	2·6	44			✓	
Jedburgh			44	✓	✓	✓	✓
Denholm			49	✓	✓	✓	✓
Hawick			55	✓	✓	✓	✓
Selkirk			57	✓		✓	✓
Abbotsford House			65			✓	
Galashiels	1·2	2·0	65	✓		✓	✓

Whether you choose a 5-day or 6-day itinerary, happily you will end each day's walk at a town or village with options for accommodation and refreshments and plenty of points of interest. The smaller places, including St Boswells and Denholm, have good facilities but limited choice. Whatever your preference and budget for accommodation, make bookings well in advance. This applies even more strongly if you are hiking in a group or at a busy time of year.

For those who intend to camp, there are commercial campsites in Melrose and Jedburgh, and also at Spital Tower near Denholm and at Hornshole Bridge, near Hawick see page 68. Wild camping can be undertaken at suitable locations along the Way, as long as your approach is self-sufficient and responsible as specified by the *Scottish Outdoor Access Code*: see pages 12 and 69. The table above summarises the main facilities.

You can book your own accommodation, based on web searches or recommendation, but if you need an early breakfast it may be wise to phone your hosts first. (Most B&Bs will cater for an early breakfast or late arrival if given notice, but you may have to negotiate a little.)

If you expect to need a packed lunch, mention that also, especially for sections such as Hawick/Selkirk with no facilities, or Kelso/Jedburgh where the only facilities are some distance off-route. In any event, take plenty of water each day, and food as needed.

At least five specialist tour operators offer to organise the complete walking package for you, including accommodation and baggage transfer: see page 68. As of 2017, there is no official website for the Borders Abbeys Way, but various independent websites provide useful information: see our page
www.rucsacs.com/links/baw.

Queen's Head hotel, Kelso

Access issues and dogs

Everyone has the right to be on most land and inland water providing they act responsibly. Your access rights and responsibilities are explained fully in the Scottish Outdoor Access Code

Whether you're in the outdoors or managing the outdoors, the key things are to
- take responsibility for your own actions
- respect the interests of other people
- care for the environment.

Find out more by visiting
www.outdooraccess-scotland.com or
by contacting Scottish Natural Heritage;
see page 69 for details.

The Scottish Outdoor Access Code interprets Scottish access rights from law. As with most of Scotland's Great Trails, the Way relies upon a management agreement between the local authority and landowners. Adopting the Code and being courteous both to landowners and to fellow route users will help everybody to maintain the route as a pleasant and sustainable experience.

When walking through farmland, please leave gates as you find them. If you have to open a gate, make sure that you close it securely behind you.

Think twice before taking your dog on the Way. You are responsible for keeping your dog under proper control at all times. Special care will be needed anywhere near livestock, and when crossing fields of crops. Never allow your dog to approach, let alone worry, livestock and if lambs or calves are around, try to avoid them by not taking your dog into that field. A farmer may suggest temporary diversions to avoid an area with young livestock: please follow local diversions.

If you go into a field of mature farm animals, keep your dog on a short lead, or at least under very close control. Keep a good distance between you and the livestock at all times and never pass between cows and their young. Cattle may be inquisitive, defensive or territorial. If cattle react aggressively to you upon entering their field, the guidance is clear: If you have a dog on a lead, let the dog off the lead and take the shortest, safest route out of the field.

When entering fields of crops, use the waymarked path and keep your dog to the path. At all times, be considerate towards other Way users. You must clean up after your dog if it defecates in a public open place. During the breeding season (usually April-July) keep your dog on a short lead or close at heel to avoid disturbing birds that nest on or near the ground.

Even if your dog is a paragon of obedience and serenity, think about how it may limit your choices of accommodation and refreshments. Many accommodation hosts do not accept dogs, however well-behaved, and others impose extra conditions and charges. Remember that the Way includes some stiles that your dog will have to climb or be lifted over.

Cycling

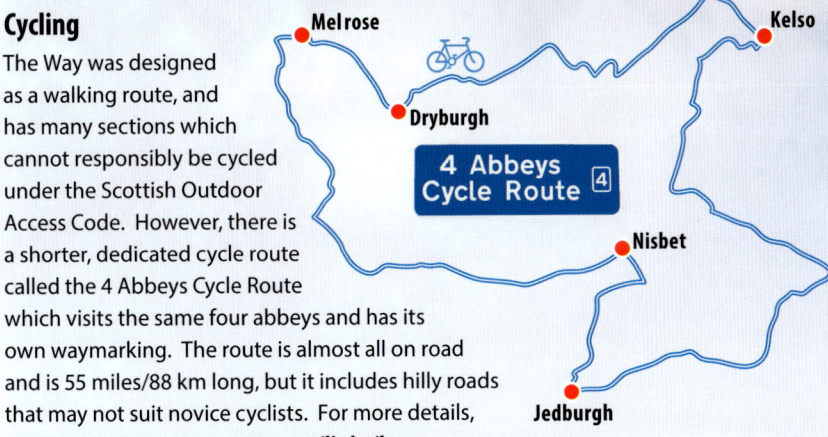

The Way was designed as a walking route, and has many sections which cannot responsibly be cycled under the Scottish Outdoor Access Code. However, there is a shorter, dedicated cycle route called the 4 Abbeys Cycle Route which visits the same four abbeys and has its own waymarking. The route is almost all on road and is 55 miles/88 km long, but it includes hilly roads that may not suit novice cyclists. For more details, visit our page *www.rucsacs.com/links/baw*.

Common Ridings

Each year, towns and villages in the Borders celebrate the history of the reiver (raider) with vibrant Common Ridings: see page 17. Each festival includes large-scale horse ridings throughout the weeklong event (in Jedburgh, two weeks). If walking the Way during these festivities, be prepared for lively events and huge pressure on accommodation within the towns.

Selected Common Ridings and festivals

March	Hawick Reivers Festival
early June	Hawick Common Riding
mid June	Selkirk Common Riding
mid/late June	Borders Book Festival, Melrose Festival Week
late June/early July	Galashiels Braw Lads Gathering
late June/early July	Jethart Callants Festival (Jedburgh, two weeks)
late July	Kelso Civic Week (including Common Riding)

For more events and details visit: *www.returntotheridings.co.uk*

What to bring

Experienced walkers will already know what they think worth carrying on a long walk, but beginners may appreciate a starting-point. We divide our checklist into essential and desirable, knowing that opinions will differ. With experience, you soon learn what matters most to you. The list omits overnight sleepwear, and changes of clothing generally: it focuses on what you need to walk comfortably and safely.

Packing for a long walk is always a compromise. You need to stay warm and dry in all weathers, to be fed and watered and to know where you are, but try to avoid unduly heavy loads. Many people end up carrying far more than they really need 'just in case'. Consider using a local baggage transfer service, but remember that you still need to carry enough drinking water (or means of purification), food and clothing to stay warm and dry each day.

The local economy which relies upon visitors is really helped when you spend money along the Way. Many B&Bs cannot accept credit, debit or contactless cards, so we recommend you take plenty of cash, especially if you don't have cheques drawn on a British bank. Cash machines (ATMs) are available in Melrose, Newtown St Boswells, Kelso, Jedburgh, Hawick and Selkirk and some shops will let you take 'cashback' along with a purchase.

Packing checklist

The checklist below provides a starting point for your packing. Normally you will be wearing the first three or four items and carrying the rest in your rucksack.

Essential

- waterproof rucksack cover or liner(s)
- comfortable, waterproof walking boots
- specialist walking socks
- waterproof jacket and over-trousers
- clothing in layers (tops, trousers, jacket)
- gaiters
- hat (for warmth and/or sun protection)
- guidebook and compass
- water carrier and plenty of water (or purification tablets)
- enough food to last between supply points
- first aid kit, including blister treatment
- toilet tissue (preferably biodegradable)
- personal toiletries
- insect repellent and sun protection

Desirable

- walking poles
- whistle and torch: *essential* if you are walking alone or in winter
- plenty of spare socks
- gloves
- camera
- plenty of spare batteries and memory cards for camera
- binoculars – useful for watching wildlife
- notebook and pen
- pouch or secure pockets for keeping small items handy and safe
- mobile phone.

> Mobile phone coverage is generally good throughout the Way, with weak or no signal in places, depending on your network provider. Never rely on a mobile for personal safety. If you run out of battery, signal or credit (or if the phone is flooded or lost), you need to be able to cope.

Camping

Camping is the ultimate low-cost, self-sufficient approach to long-distance walking. It is also much more demanding than having a soft bed and somewhere indoors to dry out wet clothing each night. You will certainly be carrying much heavier loads: at minimum, a tent, sleeping bag and mat, food, stove, fuel, cooking utensils and you need a much larger rucksack (50-90 litres) to contain it all. It would be unwise to embark on this without previous experience, and some who camp are glad to use a baggage transfer service. However, this has to be pre-booked, which negates the flexibility of deciding how far to walk before pitching your tent.

2·1 History

King David I

The key figure in the history of the Borders abbeys was David I, King of Scotland from 1124-1153. He was the son of King Malcolm III and the English princess, Margaret. Born in Scotland in about 1082, David was exiled to England when his uncle Donald III became king. He then spent much of his youth in England and adopted many of the ideas brought there by the Normans.

In 1124 he returned to Scotland as king, and became a great moderniser, setting up burghs such as Berwick and Roxburgh and introducing Scotland's first coinage. The burghs, based on existing settlements, were defended by castles, with defined boundaries and trading rights.

King David reorganised the Scottish church, creating new bishoprics and founding abbeys. He founded his first abbey at Selkirk in 1113 even before he became king. Nothing now remains of it because within 15 years the monks had moved to Kelso to obtain protection from the neighbouring castle at Roxburgh. All four of the main Borders abbeys visited by this route were founded during David's reign: Kelso in 1128, Melrose in 1136, Jedburgh in 1138 and Dryburgh in 1150.

Monasticism was very important during the Middle Ages. Abbeys were centres of learning at a time when few people were educated and life was often hard and brutal. Many abbeys had schools attached, and they also had strong links with the early universities. Monks played an important role in medicine, and most abbeys had pharmacies. They had connections with abbeys in other countries and were open to international ideas.

Dryburgh Abbey

The abbeys also had economic importance. Monks practised farming and were expected to be self-sufficient. Unfortunately, over time many monastic communities became corrupted by the great wealth bestowed on them by many donors. By the 16th century monasticism had fallen into widespread disrepute.

As you can see from their ruins, abbeys were complex institutions. In addition to the church there were dormitories where the monks slept, communal kitchens and dining areas (refectories), areas for study, communal lavatories and so forth. Each monk's day was carefully regulated from a very early start with prayers to a late ending, also with prayers. In between, periods of time were set aside for work, study and meals. The routines varied depending on the order to which the monks belonged. David favoured orders from France, such as the Cistercians (Melrose) and the Tironensians (Kelso).

All of the Borders abbeys suffered recurring damage from repeated English invasions. Their end came with the Reformation of 1560. The new Protestant church had no use for monks, and the abbeys were dissolved and fell into ruin.

King David I was responsible for the founding of all of the Borders abbeys. Nothing survives of Selkirk, but the other four can be visited while walking the Way. For information about Melrose, Dryburgh, Kelso and Jedburgh Abbeys, see the following pages: 28, 34, 39 and 46. For details of opening times and for the Historic Environment Scotland Explorer Pass, see page 68.

The Borders reivers

The lands to the north and south of the Border were in constant turmoil between the 13th and 17th centuries, with the English and Scottish armies striving for dominance. Even when not at war, the area was turbulent and largely lawless.

The Borders area was mostly open hill and moorland, unsuitable for arable crops but good for grazing livestock. Rearing and tending sheep, cattle and goats was essential to survival. The turbulent times encouraged communities and families towards a predatory existence; loyalty to a powerful clan became more important than abiding by the law.

Reivers

The reiver (or raider) was a product of the times, and clan names such as Armstrong, Bell, Crozier, Graham, Johnston, Kerr, Maxwell, Nixon, Robson and Scott were well known for organised feuding, pillaging, cattle rustling, arson and murder on both sides of the Border. These activities were an accepted part of daily life, seen as necessary to survival.

Reivers wore steel bonnets, partly armoured quilted jackets and thick leather riding boots with spurs. They rode on small, agile ponies. Whilst they had many weapons, they preferred the 'lang spear' (8-12 feet long).

Statues that celebrate the Hornshole skirmish

Only after 1603, with the Union of the Crowns of England and Scotland, did peace come to the Borders. Following a massive reiver raid into Cumbria, James VI of Scotland (now also James I of England) set about clearing the area of the 'rebels and disorderly'. In 1605 many reivers were executed or banished from the area. By the early 17th century, probably for the first time in history, the Borders became peaceful.

Common Ridings

Throughout reiving times, in order to protect the clan's boundaries or 'marches' a leading townsman would be appointed to ride around the perimeter of their territory to protect the common lands from neighbouring clans. This practice is commemorated annually in each of the Border towns as part of the Common Riding festivals.

Hawick's Common Riding marks the start of festivities. It commemorates the historic capture of the English flag in the famous Hornshole skirmish in 1514: see photo above and page 53. For dates of the Common Ridings, see **www.returntotheridings.co.uk**.

Fording the Jed Water

2·2 Geology and scenery

The Scottish Borders is a vast area covering over 1080 square miles (2800 sq km). The Way takes you through many landscapes within the central Borders: the majestic Eildon Hills, the meandering valleys of the Rivers Tweed and Teviot, the upland areas of Black Law, Rubers Law, Wollrig, Drinkstone Hill, the Selkirk Hills, Whitlaw Kips – all of them providing wide vistas – and the appealing Cauldshiels Loch. The Way also offers expansive panoramas of the surrounding hills, including the Liddesdales, Cheviots, Tweedsmuirs and Moorfoots. In between lie many attractive fields, open moorland, broadleaf woodland and rolling hills.

The geology of this land is fascinating. Much can be learned from an area sandwiched between the rounded Lammermuir Hills (made from an ancient ocean floor) and the Cheviots (made of granite). Between these two ranges of hills, land was gouged out by the glaciers of the Ice Age and the subsequent thaw. This formed the valleys of the Tweed and its tributaries.

River Tweed

Scotland was once part of a huge continent that included Greenland and North America. About 400 million years ago this collided with the European continent (including England). Each continent brought with it muds, silts and sands scraped from the seabed. The sediments were metamorphosed into greywacke – a dark, hard type of sandstone. Where squeezed together, the two continents were uplifted and folded to form the basis of the Southern Uplands.

During the Devonian period (400-360 million years ago) the whole area was an arid desert. Rapid erosion by periodic river flows created the Old Red Sandstones of the area and the distinctive red soil.

From 360-290 million years ago there were many volcanic eruptions across the area. This first created the Cheviots Hills including White Law, The Schill, Auchope Cairn and King's Seat. Later volcanos formed the Eildon Hills near Melrose, Black Hill at Earlston, Sandy Knowes (on which Smailholm Tower stands), Dunion Hill, Black Law and Peniel Heugh near Jedburgh, and Rubers Law and Bonchester Hill near Hawick.

The Eildon Hills – the most complex volcano – was formed of hard igneous rock. The lava barely surfaced, but rather cooled underground instead, forming sills. Later eruptions threw huge blocks of rock and ash into the air. Nature has since opened the volcano up and the layers in the present day hills can still be seen clearly.

During most of the last 2 million years, the area was covered by massive ice sheets, hundreds of metres thick, shifting from south-west to north-east. The ice sheet, filled with boulders, scoured and moulded the land, resulting in many east-west ridges and oval mounds dotted across the landscape. Many of the craggy volcanic hills have a 'tail' to the east: created by the ice sheet stripping away softer rock around the front and sides as it advanced and leaving a long gradual ridge, which was protected from the impact of the moving ice.

About 15,000 years ago the ice sheets began to melt. The thawing ice created huge flows of water, especially around the edges of the ice sheets. The water eventually created many cleughs (steep ravines), river valleys and natural lochs. The meandering water also dumped boulders, gravel, mud and sand in its path. In times of flood, the overflowing rivers dumped their debris, forming vast alluvial plains. Many of the Border towns were built on these plains because their soils and gradients are excellent for agriculture.

As the ice sheets withdrew, much of the area gradually became covered in oak, elm and hazel woodlands. About 10,000 years ago, human impact slowly started to change the landscape as forests were cleared to allow grazing for livestock. More recently, suitable land was turned to cultivation, and therefore drainage and soils were improved.

Scott's view towards the Eildons

2·3 Habitats and wildlife

Small tortoiseshell

If you are keen to spot wildlife, carry binoculars and walk alone or with walkers who share your interest and will move quietly. Try to set off soon after sunrise, or go for a stroll in the evening, when animals are more active than in the daytime. Midges also prefer these times, so protect your skin, especially between May and September and in still weather.

The Borders Abbeys Way runs through four main habitat types:
- lowland farm and meadows
- rivers and riverbanks
- woodland and forestry
- upland farm and hillside.

Lowland farm and meadows

Low-lying farmland is rich in wildlife, as well as its more obvious livestock. Brown hares are shy mammals that you may spot, if you're lucky, chasing each other across the fields or even 'boxing'. Although swift on the run, hares rely mainly on their ability to stay completely still, concealed by camouflage, to escape detection by predators.

Brown hare

Mature hedgerows are a feature of farmland, rich in wild flowers and supporting a diversity of insects. In summer, the colour range is amazing – deep purple meadow cranesbill, yellow ragwort and red campion.

Yellowhammer, female. Inset: wren

They produce seeds and sustain insects that in turn nourish many lovely small birds, including wrens, dunnocks, linnets and the endangered yellowhammer. The male is brownish with a contrasting yellow head and distinctive pleading song, whereas females are more stripey yellow all over.

Skylark

Farmland is also home to the enchanting skylark, albeit you will see them also on higher moorland. Its colouring is streaky brownish, with cream underparts, and on the ground it can be difficult to spot. However, its soaring, near-vertical display flight is breathtaking and unmistakable. Above all, its melodious trilling song evokes the essence of spring.

In summer months, many species of butterfly flutter around the meadows and farms. Two of the more colourful are the Small tortoiseshell, with its warm orange wings patterned with black and white, and the Peacock with decorations that mimic the 'eyes' of a peacock wing. The Common blue also thrives on unimproved grassland.

Common blue (male)

Otter

Rivers and riverbanks

The Rivers Tweed and Teviot and their banks are a strong feature of the Way. After centuries of damage by humans, some strong ecology projects have been rewarded by good results. Invasive species such as giant hogweed, Japanese knotweed and Himalayan balsam are being controlled. Pollution has been tackled and artificial barriers to spawning fish removed. Both are now healthy rivers with good stocks of salmon, brown trout and grayling. The Tweed has the highest annual total of rod-caught salmon in Scotland, and is very attractive to anglers from afar.

The same bounty of fish attracts the charming otter to these rivers. You might catch a glimpse of this shy mammal if you are out very early or late, move silently and know where to look. More likely you will see otter traces, perhaps footprints or spraint on the river bank. Otters are land animals, but their webbed feet, powerful tail and ability to close off their ears and nose are all adaptations that work well in the water. Otters are agile and effective aquatic hunters, preying on fish, water birds and amphibians.

Dipper

Goosanders are diving ducks that also feed on fish, using their long, serrated bills. The male goosander has a glossy dark green head, like a mallard drake, over a bright white body, whereas females have a red-brown head and a greyish body. Their bodies are streamlined to help when diving and catching fish. Goosanders like to live in large flocks, sometimes of up to several thousand. They make a low, harsh croak, but in the breeding season they make a soft whistling noise.

You may well see grey herons from the riverbanks. These dignified birds have a grey body supported by stilt-like legs.

Grey heron

A heron will often stand motionless in the water, patiently waiting for its next meal, before its long beak makes a lightning strike to capture an unlucky fish.

Other birds you may see around rivers include oystercatchers, grey wagtails and dippers. Oystercatchers are large black and white birds with a long orange beak. They are common near the coast where they feed on cockles and mussels; when inland they feed mainly on worms. Grey wagtails have very long tails and grey upper bodies with bright yellow underparts. Dippers are small white-throated birds, with plump brown bodies. Typically they perch on rocks in fast-flowing water, dipping their heads up and down. They feed on insect larvae and shrimps, and are skilful at hunting underwater.

Marsh marigolds are similar to buttercups, with more striking yellow flowers and larger, frilled green leaves. They flourish in wet areas and flower from March until June. Wild garlic (or Ramsons) is plentiful, easily identified by its distinctive smell. It blooms with white star shaped flowers during May and June. It is illegal to dig up the bulbs without the landowner's consent, but you can pick the leaves and stems if you are certain of your identification. Lily of the valley and Autumn crocus are poisonous, but look rather similar: beware.

Goosander female (foreground) and male

Roe deer (buck)

Woodland and forestry

Foxes are widespread in Scottish woodland. Its red-brown body has a pale underside, and its long brush-like tail helps its balance. Carnivores by preference, foxes hunt for small mammals, but they adapt to whatever food is available, including fruit, vegetables, fish, frogs and worms. Foxes tend to move stealthily through the undergrowth, and you will be lucky to spot one.

Roe deer are common, and can be seen in woodland areas and in some farmland, notably while grazing around dawn. They are generally solitary, but may form small groups in the winter. Bucks can have short straight antlers that fall off in the winter and grow back again in the spring. These deer do not have tails but small white patches at the rump, making them easy to identify.

Red squirrels are rare in the Borders, however certain pockets of mixed conifer woodland support the species. They are more delicate than their grey cousins, with distinctive hairy tufts on their ears. They are at risk from the American greys, not only because of competition for food, but also because the greys carry squirrelpox, a disease that's deadly to reds. If you sight any squirrels, red or grey, please report them online: *www.scottishsquirrels.org.uk*.

Fox

Red squirrel

Woodland in the Borders includes productive forest, often planted with fast-growing Sitka spruce. These giants can grow up to 50 metres tall. The Scots pine, Britain's only native pine tree, has a distinctive orange-brown bark with dark green needles in pairs. Larch trees are unusual among conifers in being deciduous: in winter their needles turn brown and drop.

Other deciduous trees include oak, rowan and ash. Oak trees have leaves that grow in bunches with distinctive scalloped edges. Their acorns ripen in the autumn and drop off. The trunk of a rowan tree is a smooth and may be silvery, with leaves in pairs and a rich red berry-like fruit. Ash trees can be mistaken for rowan, but they grow much larger – up to 40 metres tall, whereas rowans grow up to 10 metres.

The woodland floor is home to many wildflowers in summer, including wood sorrel, which has heart-shaped trefoil leaves and frail, five-petalled, white flowers. The Scottish primrose is a rare flower with five heart-shaped petals, their vibrant purple contrasting with the yellow centre. Red campion has hairy leaves and stems, with heart-shaped petals of a deep pink-red. The delicate harebell, also known as the Scottish bluebell, does well in woodland shade, but it also thrives on exposed hillsides and grassland.

Bluebell woodland; inset harebell

Upland farm and hillside

The Borders is home to small birds of prey including kestrels and sparrowhawks, but the one you are most likely to see is the buzzard, either over higher ground or farm fields. Typically buzzards soar with their wings held in a shallow V-shape, with tail fanned out; they also sometimes perch on fence posts. The buzzard's wingspan ranges from 1·1- 1·35 metres (43-53 inches), whereas that of the golden eagle (which you are extremely unlikely to see) is 2 metres or more. Buzzard wings are broad and curved, varying in colour from very dark to light brown, but always with dark wing-tips. Its melancholy mewing sounds similar to a cat, and is heard mainly in the spring.

Red grouse

You may see and hear skylarks over high ground as well as over lower farmland. The hills are home also to many small birds including wheater and meadow pipits – and the cuckoo which is a brood parasite that targets meadow pipits and dunnocks.

Heather grows in abundance across the moorlands, including the Eildon Hills, in late summer carpeting the hillside with colours ranging from pale pink to deep purple. Most of this is common heather, but on the south-facing slopes of the Eildons, it gives way to bell heather. Heather moorland supports red grouse – a plump game bird which depends on heather not only for food but also for nesting sites. It has become scarce on the Eildons, but may be in the process of returning from higher ground.

Many flowers and plants flourish on the high grounds. Gorse is a spiny shrub that flourishes in poor soil and bears masses of golden yellow flowers with a pleasing coconut smell. Although it can flower in almost any frost-free month, it can paint certain hills a striking yellow in April/May.

Tormentil has a glossy yellow four-petalled flower, and clumps of tormentil are an important source of nectar for bees. The Devil's-Bit Scabious is also widespread. Wild orchids are flowers that use amazing visual devices to attract fertilisation by insect visitors. Two fairly widespread species are the Common spotted orchid and Northern marsh orchid, and in acidic soil the Heath spotted orchid.

Common spotted orchid

3 Tweedbank to Melrose

From Tweedbank station, you can reach the centre of Melrose by bus. There are at least three buses per hour and it takes about seven minutes to reach the stop in Buccleuch Street, less than 100 m from Melrose Abbey.

- However, the 3-km riverside walk to Melrose makes a pleasant preamble. Start with your back to the station and follow a tarmac cycle path signed 'Melrose 1·75 miles'. After 500 m bear left at the green Southern Upland Way sign and descend to the B6374 main road.

- Cross over and on its far side descend through a timber gate at a fingerpost to join the Borders Abbeys Way. Go down a narrow path, past an information board for Skirmish Hill: see panel.

Skirmish Hill

Skirmish Hill is the site of the Battle of Melrose in July 1526. The struggle was over the custody of the young King James V, then only 14 years old. A force of Scotts and Elliots attempted to rescue James from Archibald Douglas, Earl of Angus, and his Ker allies. Although the rescue failed, the Ker chief was killed by an Elliot near the Turn Again Stone, starting a clan feud that lasted many years.

- Join the banks of the River Tweed, from which the cloth 'tweed' accidentally derived its name. The river rises from the Tweed's Well at Tweedsmuir and reaches the North Sea at Berwick-upon-Tweed. Anglers from far and wide come here to cast flies for salmon and trout.

- Continue downstream, passing the grounds of a large hotel and later leaving the bank briefly at a timber waymarker (thistle in a hexagon). After passing through a gate, you join a road fleetingly, then descend a flight of steps to resume the river bank.

- After 1·7 km of riverside walking, near the weir, a fingerpost points to the route continuing along the bank (signed Southern Upland Way). For the facilities of Melrose we suggest you leave the Way here and turn off right (south) at another fingerpost (with a blue E2 disc) signed 'Melrose Town Centre'.

- Follow the tarmac path uphill, with Melrose Parish Church on your right, until it meets St Mary's Road. Cross over and follow the tarmac path straight ahead through the small park, with Melrose Rugby Football Club on your left.

- Reach the B6374 main road and turn left along it. After 200 m, the High Street forks: the direct route to Melrose Abbey bears left along Buccleuch Street for 180 m, and turns left at its end into Abbey Street. The abbey stands on your right, about 50 m downhill.

- Should you need to detour for the shops in the town centre, instead keep to the right fork of the High Street to reach the main square. From here, turn left into Abbey Street and follow it for 200 m to Melrose Abbey.

Melrose

Melrose is a picturesque market town sandwiched between the River Tweed and the distinctive Eildon Hills, the site of a vast Roman fort, Trimontium. The town is the home of the famous 'Melrose Sevens' rugby tournament and its attractions include Priorwood Gardens, Harmony Gardens, the Trimontium Museum and Melrose Abbey. Priorwood Gift Shop, next to the abbey, houses a VisitScotland iCentre: see page 68.

Melrose, first referred to as *Mailros*, dates back to the early 12th century, directly evolving from the prosperous business of Melrose Abbey. This was the first Cistercian abbey in Scotland, founded in 1136 by King David I and built by the 'white' Cistercian monks from Rievaulx in Yorkshire.

Over the centuries the abbey was ravaged by conflict, notably by Edward II in 1322, but later rebuilt by King Robert the Bruce. The abbey was again destroyed in 1385 by Richard II, and later rebuilt again. It was finally ruined beyond full repair in 1544 as part of King Henry VIII's 'Rough Wooing', which focused on Mary Queen of Scots.

The abbey is one of the most beautiful monastic ruins in Britain. Visit it to enjoy its gothic architecture and unusual sculptures including mischievous goblins, cooks and a bagpipe-playing pig. The Chapter House is believed to still contain Robert the Bruce's heart and there is a rich array of medieval objects in the museum. The abbey is open daily and is cared for by Historic Environment Scotland: see page 68.

3·1 Melrose to Kelso

| | | 32 | 36 | 37 |

Distance 17·9 miles 28·8 km
Terrain quiet country roads, farm tracks, woodland and riverside paths
Grade main route has a modest total ascent of 265 m/870 ft, mainly in the climbs to Eildon Mains and Old Dalcove; the alternative route includes a steep climb to Eildon Hill North (404 m/1325 ft), rewarded by stunning views
Food & drink Melrose (wide choice), Newtown St Boswells, St Boswells, Kelso (wide choice)
Summary long and interesting first section, which many will prefer to split into two, leaving time to explore the Eildon Hills and Dryburgh Abbey; to overnight in St Boswells means going slightly offroute (0·9 mi/1·5 km each way)

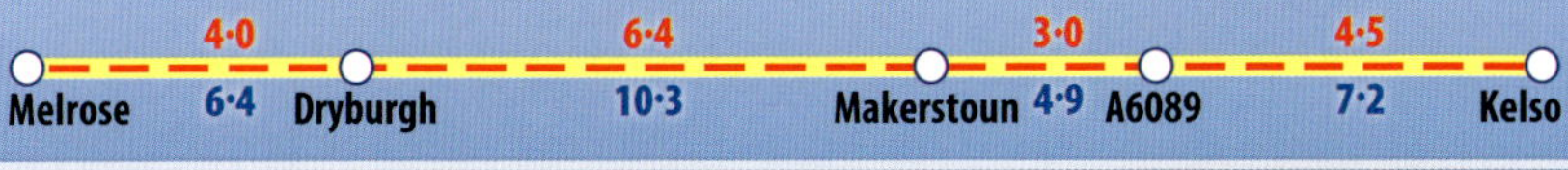

Melrose — 6·4 — Dryburgh — 10·3 — Makerstoun — 4·9 — A6089 — 7·2 — Kelso
4·0   6·4   3·0   4·5

- From Melrose Abbey head south a short distance up Abbey Street to Priorwood Gardens, a former part of the abbey grounds, and now open to the public.
- Immediately, you face a choice of routes. The main Way continues by turning left off Abbey Street here: resume directions from the middle of page 31, whilst the Eildon Hills alternative begins on page 30.

Marker for Robert the Bruce's buried heart

Melrose Abbey

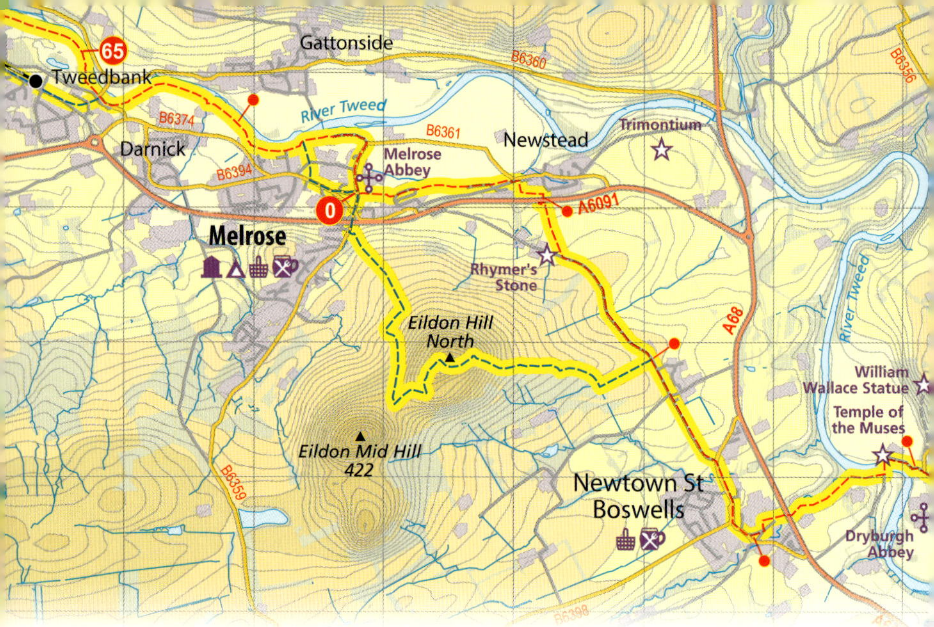

The Eildon Hills alternative is slightly longer, much more strenuous and not as clearly waymarked as the Way, but it affords better views. Start by following the waymarked Eildon Hills Walk (also shared with St Cuthbert's Way) and rejoin the trail after 2 miles, at Eildon Mains: see map above.

Continue up Abbey Street into the Market Square and cross the road following Dingleton Road. This is where the Eildon Hills climb begins.

Pass under the bypass and follow the road uphill. After 100 m turn left down stone steps and cross a small burn to enter coniferous woodland.

Follow the path and climb the long flight of timber steps that awaits. There are 133 steps, however there is a convenient bench half way up the ascent if a rest is required. Continue the climb uphill between fields, onto open hill.

Veer right following the St Cuthbert's Way and the fence line through the gorse until reaching an open grassy area.

North over the Eildons

Turn left, climbing steeply, following the path towards another bench where views across Melrose, the River Tweed, and Galashiels to the west and Berwickshire to the east can be appreciated.

A further climb to the saddle between Eildon Mid Hill and Eildon Hill North will reveal fine views to the south. Eildon Mid Hill is the highest of the three hills, but our route turns left to follow the grassy path to the summit of Eildon Hill North. The views here are panoramic and provide an overview of the Borders Abbeys Way countryside – Kelso to the east, Jedburgh to the south-east, Hawick to the south and Selkirk to the south-west. Looking down the southern face of the hill, you will also see the ramparts of a Bronze Age hill fort inhabited around 1000 BC.

Continue past the collapsed cairn and descend on the eastern side of the hill following the steep grassy pathway down to the foot of the hill. Continue across the field to the south-eastern corner and exit into deciduous woodland by the gate. Turn left and follow the wide woodland track downhill.

Pass the water station on the left and at the track junction turn left to continue along a tree-lined path, with a field on your right. Upon reaching the road, at Eildon Mains, turn right and follow the road downhill for 1 km until you reach Newtown St Boswells.

- To follow the main Way, turn left off Abbey Street at Priorwood Gardens into a lane, and continue along this path with great views of the abbey to your left. Continue through the public park and across Malthouse Burn to reach a road (Priorswalk) where you bear left.

- After 150 m, the Way leaves the road along a narrow path beside houses. Follow this path for 750 m until you reach the small village of Newstead.

Newstead is said to be the oldest continually inhabited settlement in Scotland, with populations recorded since 650 AD. It was strategically important throughout its history, notably for the Roman Army. Intermittently between 80 – 211 AD, the Romans settled in the large Trimontium ('three hills') camp. The site is east of the village, and there are interpretation boards but nothing recognisable remains above the ground. The village also housed many stonemasons and architects associated with Melrose Abbey.

- Dean Road takes you into the village at a road junction, where you turn right uphill onto a tree-lined path. Follow it around to the left, then turn right (south) to pass under the old railway bridge and main road (A6091).

- Upon leaving the underpass, follow the path that goes right for 50 m, then backtracks left. Turn right to pick up a hedge-lined farm track heading south towards the Eildon Hills. After 400 m, you reach the old road: now closed to vehicles, this was once the main road between Melrose and Newtown St Boswells.

- Turn left along the road, passing the site of the Rhymer's Stone. The stone was erected in 1929 to mark the site of the Eildon Tree, where (according to legend) Thomas the Rhymer met the Faerie Queen. Rhymer was a 13th century laird who famously predicted the death of King Alexander III, and was said to have supernatural powers. The site offers great views towards Leaderfoot and Black Hill.

- Follow the road as it meanders round the edge of the Eildon Hills climbing for 1 km to Eildon Mains, where the Eildon Hills alternative rejoins the main Way.

- Continue for a further 900 m along the road to reach a T-junction. Turn right to follow the B6398 road into Newtown St Boswells, with some shops on the left. The village is normally quiet, but on market days you may notice livestock and farmers going to and from the livestock market nearby.

- Pass the shops and pub, then bear left into Tweedside Road. After 150 m turn left after the houses to join St Cuthbert's Way.

- Follow the road downhill and pass under the road bridge carrying the A68 to reach the deciduous woodland of Newtown Glen.

Dryburgh Bridge

- The glen has a wide variety of trees including oak, ash and elder, and a range of wild flowers.
- Continue across the Bowden Burn heading straight through the wood. After you climb a flight of steps, the River Tweed comes into view.
- Follow the path to a viewing area which offers superb views of the river, the William Wallace statue and the surrounding countryside. Follow the path which descends to reach Dryburgh Bridge (about 800 m after the A68).
- If splitting this section over two days, you will probably overnight in St Boswells, which lies south of the river, reached by staying on the St Cuthbert's Way for a further 1·5 km. The next day, retrace your steps to Dryburgh Bridge to resume the Way.
- The main route leaves St Cuthbert's Way to cross the Tweed by Dryburgh Bridge. On its far side, look up to the left and visit the Temple of the Muses ❶.
- Afterwards, with your back to the temple, follow the tarmac lane uphill beside the river for 350 m to a road junction. To continue the Way, go straight ahead and after 220 m reach the entrance to Dryburgh Abbey: see page 34.

The Temple of the Muses
The Temple of the Muses is dedicated to local author and poet James Thomson (1700-1748), famous for writing 'The Seasons' (a cycle of four poems) and the lyrics of 'Rule Britannia'. The sandstone gazebo can be reached by a short flight of steps from the roadway. It was built in 1817 and used to house a stone statue of the Apollo Belvedere with nine muses. These were replaced in 2002 with bronze figures of the Four Seasons.

To detour to the William Wallace statue ❷, at the road junction above, instead turn left and continue uphill. After 250 m, turn left off the road at a fingerpost. Follow the path through the wood for 500 m to reach the statue, which stands 30 feet tall. Erected in 1814, it commemorates William Wallace (1270-1305). Retrace your footsteps to resume the Way.

Dryburgh Abbey

Approved by King David I, Dryburgh Abbey was founded in 1150 through an agreement between Hugh de Morville, Lord of Lauderdale and Constable of Scotland, and the White Canons. The abbey grew, and its quiet monastic existence continued until the early 13th century when ambitious rebuilding costs and a lack of income resulted in mounting debt. Over the coming years, the monastery's struggle attracted donations from many, including King David I.

Dryburgh fell victim, together with neighbouring abbeys, to Edward II, who burnt it down in 1322. After being restored, the abbey was destroyed again in 1385 and once more in the 'Rough Wooing' in 1544. The abbey finally succumbed to the Scottish Reformation of 1560.

Three prominent Scots are laid to rest in the grounds, The 11th Earl of Buchan, who bought the land in 1786; the novelist and antiquarian Sir Walter Scott of Abbotsford in 1832 (see page 66); and Field-Marshal Earl Haig of Bemersyde in 1928.

The abbey ruins display fine gothic architecture, and its setting among yew and cedar trees makes for a relaxing ambience. You can still make out the remains of the brethren homes, cloister and presbytery. The chapter house still retains its original plaster and paintwork. It is cared for by Historic Environment Scotland and is open daily: see page 68 for visit information.

River Tweed near Mertoun

- On leaving the abbey, bear right along an avenue of mature trees. After about 150 m, turn left down a path that descends to rejoin the River Tweed.
- The path continues beside the river, with St Boswells Golf Course on the opposite bank.
- After 1·2 km leave the river bank with a short climb through mixed woodland. Pass into a field and continue along its edge, with glimpses of Mertoun Bridge further downstream.
- Exit the field and turn left, climbing to Mertoun Cemetery to reach the B6356 road. Walk with care, looking out for vehicles on this stretch of road.
- After 270 m, the road bends right through Clintmains, then descends for 250 m to reach the B6404 road at Mertoun House & Gardens.
- Cross the road with care and turn left along its verge. After 330 m, turn right briefly on a farm track then go immediately left to follow the path through woodland, parallel to the road.
- At the end of the woodland, turn right down the quiet farm road, flanked by mature trees, to Magdalene Hall. Descend on the farm track to meet the River Tweed.
- Continue downstream, passing through agricultural lands of the Mertoun Estate. After 1·3 km, leave the quiet river bank and climb towards a house on the hill. This is Old Dalcove, once the site of a medieval tower house, commanding good views across the valley.

Farmland near Magdalene Hall

- Follow the track until you meet the minor road, where there are panoramic views towards Smailholm Tower, the River Tweed, Eildon Hills, Peniel Heugh and the Cheviot Hills.
- Turn right to follow the road which passes through Dalcove Mains, bending this way and that. After 0·9 km of road, turn right briefly to descend on a track, veering left and reaching a road after 1·6 km.
- At the road, bear left and follow the road to the junction at Makerstoun War Memorial. Turn right and continue along the minor road flanked with hedging for 900 m. To the right there are wide views across the rolling countryside towards the Cheviot Hills.
- At the next junction, make a left-right dogleg to pass Haymount Farm and the row of cottages to the main road (B6397).
- Cross the road with care, and continue ahead on the road past the converted farm steading to Wester Muirdean. Continue ahead along a farm track to meet the main road about 2 km after the B6397, with Skinlaws at the junction ❶.
- Cross the A6089 main road with care, and follow the tree-lined avenue past cottages on your left and a postbox on your right.
- About 190 m after the postbox, turn right opposite the gate in the wall onto a field track. Follow it downhill to meet the road (B6364).
- Cross the road and enter the field opposite through a gate. Veer left to follow the field edge, then turn right around a hilly knoll (Kaim Knowes). Cross into another field and follow its edge, turning left into an old lane.
- At the end of the lane turn right up to Berryhill on the brow of the hill. Drop down along the avenue of poplar trees towards Kelso Racecourse, on the outskirts of Kelso itself.

- At the junction, the James Thomson Memorial is prominent in the distance to the left, commemorating the author and poet who lived nearby.
- Turn right, and after 300 m left, into Golf Course Road. Follow this road around to the right and arrive opposite the recent Kelso High School.
- At the junction with the A6089, turn left and follow the pavement. After 270 m turn right onto a narrow tarmac path opposite Kelso Ice Rink.
- Follow the path through housing for about 400 m, eventually dropping down to Croft Road. Turn right and follow the road for 500 m to reach Edinburgh Road. Turn left around the perimeter wall of Floors Castle ❷: see panel.
- Follow the pavement for 150 m, then turn right into Roxburgh Street. Just as you pass the entrance signs for Floors Castle, turn right down to follow the Cobby Riverside Walk along the Tweed.
- Follow the river bank for 500 m, then make a left-right dogleg to resume Roxburgh Street. Continue into Kelso Square with the *Kelsae Stane* on your left. Go along the street to reach the gates of Kelso Abbey on your left.

> **Floors Castle**
>
> Floors Castle was built in the 1720s by William Adam and is the seat of the Ker family, Duke of Roxburghe. Its name probably derives from the original building on the site, which was the House of Floris, on the banks of the Tweed. Floors Castle and Gardens offer the opportunity to explore the history of the castle, the art, tapestries and artefacts housed within and the vast manicured grounds that surround it. For visit information, see www.floorscastle.com.

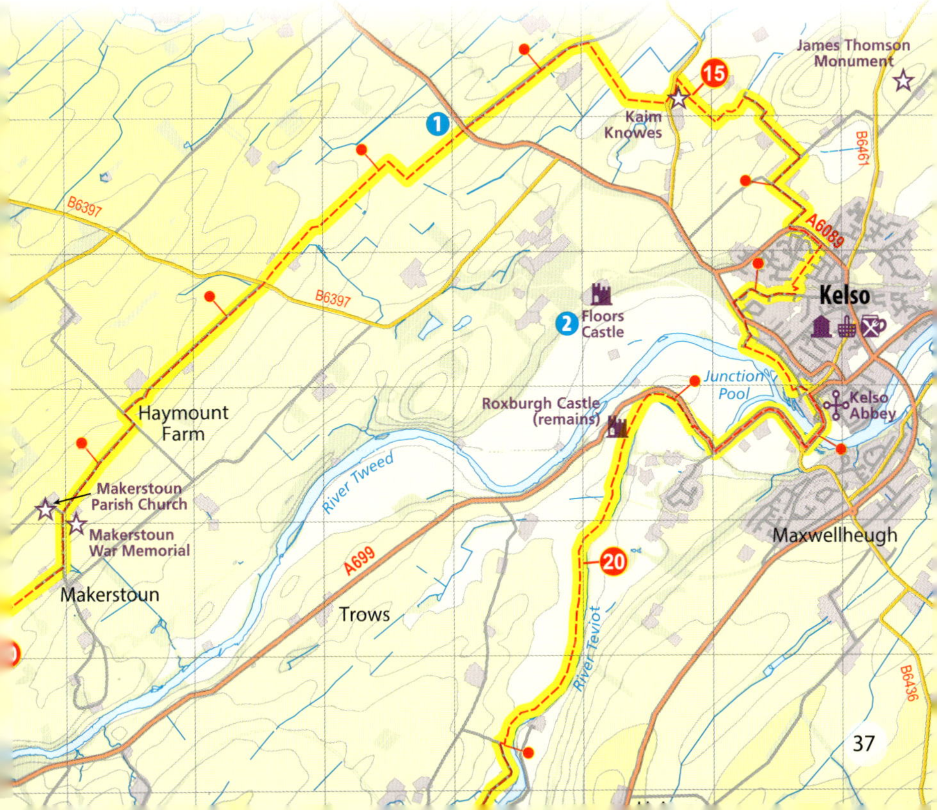

3•2 Kelso to Jedburgh

41 44

Distance 13·0 miles 20·9 km
Terrain riverside paths, disused railway, farm tracks and quiet country roads
Grade a relatively flat section along the River Teviot with a climb to Mount Ulston, total ascent 205 m/670 ft
Food & drink Kelso (wide choice), Jedburgh (wide choice)
Summary easy-going section taking in the attractive banks of the River Teviot and a long walk along an old railway line, finishing with the approach to Jedburgh below sandstone cliffs by the Jed Water

Kelso — 3·6 / 5·8 — Roxburgh — 4·5 / 7·2 — Nisbet — 4·9 / 7·9 — Jedburgh

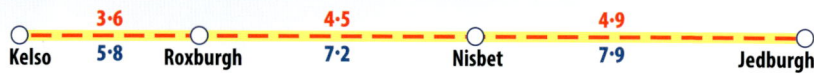

Kelso (formerly Kelsae) is a picturesque town near the junction of two rivers, the Tweed and the Teviot. Its fine six-arched bridge over the Tweed was designed by John Rennie. The town's large market square has a bull-ring set into its cobbles. The *Kelsae Stane* was designed by local sculptor Jake Harvey, unveiled in 2014. This huge 33-tonne cobble is inscribed with local placenames handwritten by local people of all ages. The handsome town hall houses a VisitScotland iCentre: see page 68.

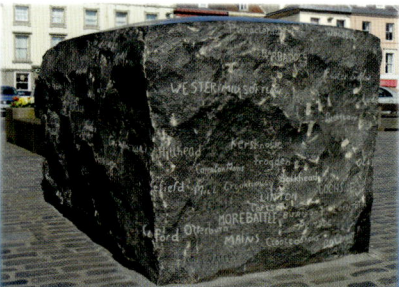

The Kelsae Stane

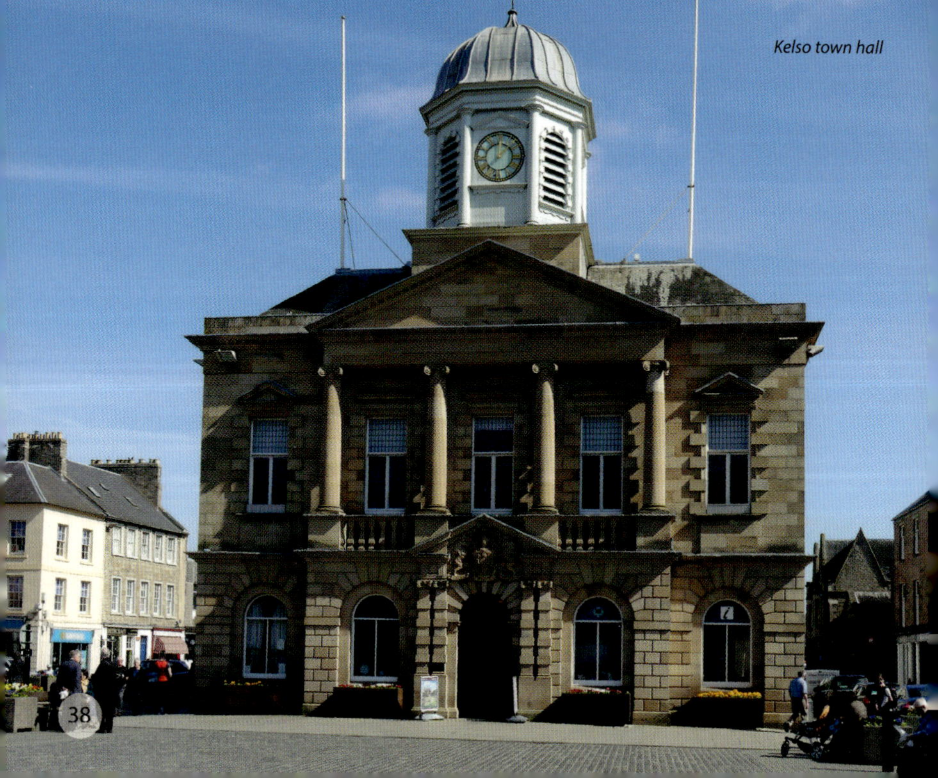

Kelso town hall

Kelso Abbey

The town developed as a result of Benedictine monks building Kelso Abbey around 1128, previously having settled in Selkirk in 1113 at King David I's invitation. The monks (Tironensians, i.e. from Tiron Abbey in northern France) were the first order to settle in Britain. They built their abbey in sight of Roxburgh Castle.

Kelso Abbey grew to be one of the wealthiest in Scotland, having control of vast areas of land. However it suffered the same fate as the other Borders abbeys.

Roxburghe Memorial Cloister, Kelso Abbey

During the 13th and early 14th centuries many battles resulted in the abbey being severely damaged, although the monks continued to repair and rebuild it. James III was crowned at the abbey in 1460, and it had a fairly peaceful life until around 1513. Further English attacks took place in 1517 and in the mid-16th century as part of the wider 'Rough Wooing'. By the 18th century, the abbey was acting as a parish kirk, many stones from the ruined buildings were removed and used in local buildings.

The west tower and nave remain standing, and the Roxburghe Memorial Cloister (restored in the 1930s) is impressive. The ruins are free to visit in daylight hours, but are closed on Thursdays and Fridays in winter: see page 68.

Kelso Abbey from the south

River Teviot near Kelso

- From Kelso Abbey, continue on the A699 pavement to cross the Tweed by the arched road bridge. At its far side, turn right to stay on the A699 beside the river and around the edge of Springwood Park, passing the Junction Pool where the Teviot joins the Tweed.
- Continue along the pavement as the road swings right over a bridge and crosses the Teviot. Keep to the pavement for a further 200 m, then turn left to pass through a gate leading to the Teviot banks.
- Turn right to continue upstream beside the river as it bends sharply left, to reach the ruins of Roxburgh Castle. Little survives of this key border fortress castle. It had eight towers, battlements and a tower house all perched upon the embankment. Flanked by the two rivers, it had a great situation, but was ravaged by war and finally succumbed to English invasions. During one recapture attempt by the Scots in 1460, James II was killed there by an exploding cannon.
- Follow this attractive stretch of river for a further 3 km passing Heiton Mill, visible on the opposite bank. Here the path leads uphill away from the river: look back for grand views towards Kelso and ahead to Roxburgh Viaduct ❷.
- Continue along the field edge and pass over a stile onto the quiet road. Turn left to follow the hedge-lined road through Roxburgh Mill Farm and into the village of Roxburgh. Ahead, you see Roxburgh Viaduct proudly spanning the River Teviot.

- On the left, look for the waymarked left turn onto a wide track down towards the river, with the viaduct prominent ahead. As you reach the river turn upstream under the vast arches of the viaduct.

Roxburgh Viaduct

- The viaduct opened in 1850 and has 15 impressive stone arches. It previously carried the Kelso railway line until its closure to trains in 1964. For great views of the River Teviot, consider a detour to the walkway across its top, reached from the path leading to Roxburgh village to the right.
- In the field to the west lie the remains of Wallace's Tower, a 16th century tower house used by the Ker family. It may have been one of the signal towers designed to warn of English attacks.
- The path continues upstream beside the river, with the grounds of Roxburgh Hotel and Golf Course on the opposite banks. There, too, are five partly hidden caves. One of these, Horse Cave, is said to have sheltered Bonnie Prince Charlie's horses while he and his army marched from Jedburgh to Kelso in 1745.
- Continue along the river bank and after a further 2 km, at the stone dyke wall, turn right to follow a field edge uphill until (within 200 m) you meet the disused Kelso – St Boswells railway.
- Turn left along the tree-lined railway for 550 m, to descend a flight of steps down to the road. Turn left at the road, then immediately right past the cottage and up the gravel track.
- The track rejoins the disused railway trackbed, making for an easy pleasant walk to the small hamlet of Nisbet, a further 4 km.
- On reaching Nisbet, turn left along the B6400 road to cross the iron bridge over the River Teviot: see photo below. On its far side, turn immediately right down the steps to join the river's south bank through the fields.
- Follow the waymarkers beside the river until eventually you meet a track. Bear right, then follow the track around to the left to resume the line of the disused railway.
- Stay on this path to reach Jedfoot, where the Jed Water merges with the River Teviot, and the main road. Cross the busy A698 with great care: this is the main route to Kelso.

Iron bridge over River Teviot

Dere Street

- Follow waymarkers to join St Cuthbert's Way heading south. It runs along Dere Street – an old Roman road that once linked York to the Antonine Wall in central Scotland. Dere Street climbs on the well-defined track past the belt of trees near the brow of the hill.
- After 900 m, turn right, heading for Mount Ulston to join a single-track road downhill, bounded by mature beech trees. Mount Ulston offers great views across the countryside towards the Eildon Hills and to Peniel Heugh, where the massive Waterloo Monument sits.
- After 1·9 km of single-track road, reach a minor road and turn left, descending through the wooded valley of the Tower Burn. After a further 550 m, you meet the A68 main road.
- Turn right to cross the A68 with care, heading diagonally opposite to reach the walkway beside the Jed Water. This is a delightful path with towering red sandstone cliffs on the opposite banks displaying visible layers in the rocks laid down 370 million years ago.
- Follow the river until you reach Old Bongate, a road that takes you right across the river. After the bridge, follow the pavement round to your left to join a path that takes you underneath the A68.
- Follow the path beside the Jed Water through the parkland. To the right you may glimpse Mary Queen of Scots House beyond the A68. Pass the hump-backed 16th century Canongate Bridge and continue on the path.

Mary Queen of Scots House

- To your right Jedburgh Abbey comes into view. Stay on the path and pass under the A68 again in a right-left dogleg. Once you reach Abbey Bridge End, the entrance to Jedburgh Abbey is straight ahead.

3·3 Jedburgh to Hawick   44 48 49

Distance 13·2 miles   21·3 km
Terrain mostly riverside paths, quiet country roads and occasional farm tracks
Grade gradual climb out of Jedburgh, followed by steep climb to Black Law (320 m/1050 ft) and a lesser climb after Spital Tower (total ascent 445 m/1460 ft)
Food & drink Jedburgh (wide choice), Denholm, Hawick (wide choice)
Summary beautiful section, leading out of Jedburgh across farmland, climbing open hill to give impressive views, then descending to Denholm and following the tranquil banks of the River Teviot

Jedburgh	5·0	Bedrule	2·6	Denholm	5·6	Hawick
	8·0		4·2		9·1	

Jedburgh (formerly Jethart) is a pretty market town near the border, and a Royal and Ancient Burgh. This historic gateway to Scotland fell victim to many battles and cross border raids, and has links with many historic figures, including Mary Queen of Scots, Bonnie Prince Charlie, Robert Burns, Sir Walter Scott and William Wordsworth.

Two of its visitor attractions – Jedburgh Castle Jail (gaol) and the Mary Queen of Scots House – are free to visit, and the town also provides free wifi: **www.jedburgh.org.uk**. The Town Hall houses a VisitScotland iCentre: see page 68. Above all, the town is dominated by the exceptionally impressive ruins of Jedburgh Abbey.

Jedburgh Castle Jail

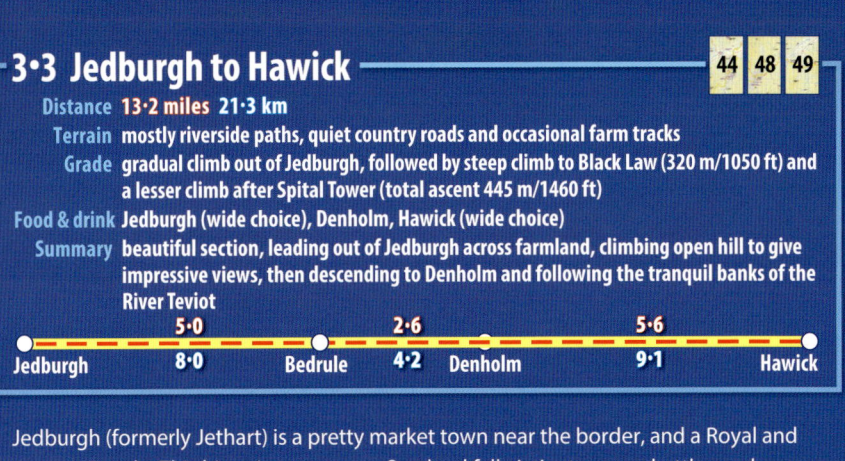

Victorian jubilee fountain, Jedburgh

Jedburgh Abbey

Jedburgh, like the other Borders abbeys, was built in the 12th century under King David I. It housed Augustinians priests, who originated from St Quentin Abbey, near Beauvais, France.

Jedburgh Abbey was prone to many attacks and ravaged by wars throughout its lifespan, particularly between 1296 and 1356 (Wars of Independence). At one stage the resident canons had to be evacuated for their own safety. In 1305 Edward I of England's troops removed the abbey's roof leading for use in their armament. Further attacks in the 15th and 16th centuries, and the Protestant Reformation of 1560, sealed its fate.

Rose window, west front

The abbey now stands as a vast ruin of unusual romanesque and early gothic architecture. The abbey church of St Mary the Virgin remains largely intact. A striking feature is the great rose window (built around 1440) in the west gable. You can still see the remains of the cloister, now reduced to ground level and the recreated cloister garden. There are also domestic buildings and its visitor centre houses various artefacts including the Jedburgh Shrine, Jedburgh Comb and gaming tokens. The abbey is now cared for by Historic Environment Scotland: for visit information, see page 68.

Jedburgh Abbey from the north-west

- Leaving Jedburgh Abbey on your left, walk uphill passing the handsome Town Hall building with iCentre on the right. At the top of Abbey Place you reach the market square with its multi-coloured buildings.

- Turn left up Castlegate for 350 m to reach, and if possible visit, Jedburgh Castle Jail: see panel.

- Turn left to follow Galahill down past a cemetery and large houses. To the left are splendid views over Jedburgh's parkland and the Jed Water valley.

- The tarmac road soon becomes a farm track. Before the last house, bear left off the main track down a narrow path, descend to cross the stream (Miller's Burn) and climb timber steps.

- Continue along the track, passing through a plantation, and pass Todlaw Farm where tarmac resumes.

Jedburgh Castle Jail and Museum
Jedburgh Castle Jail was built in 1823 on the site of a medieval castle demolished in 1409. It was designed by Archibald Elliot as a Howard Reform Prison, and is one of the finest remaining examples. The Jail closed in 1868, but it was restored and opened as a museum in 1964. The cells of the prison building still retain their original features, whilst the history of Jedburgh is presented in collections of artefacts and paintings. The Jail is open from late March to late October (Mon-Sat 10.00-16.30, Sun 13.00-16.00) and admission is free.

Track near Dunion Hill

- At the T-junction (1·3 km after the Jail), turn right to follow the track uphill. This stretch provides great views back to Jedburgh to the right, and of Dunion Hill and Black Law (with masts) ahead to the left.
- The track dips briefly to cross a burn, then climbs beside trees. After 1 km from the last junction, reach another T-junction and turn left onto an old grassy road. Look back for a wide vista across the Jed valley to the distant Cheviot hills.
- Follow the old road through fields with gate/stiles (gates often open). It leads through a plantation with large boulders stacked alongside the track.
- Exit the plantation and keep ahead along the left side of a large field, which presents vast views south-west across the farmland to the distant border.
- Continue through the fields, descending gently parallel to the fence. At a gate/stile, turn right to descend into Merlin Dean.

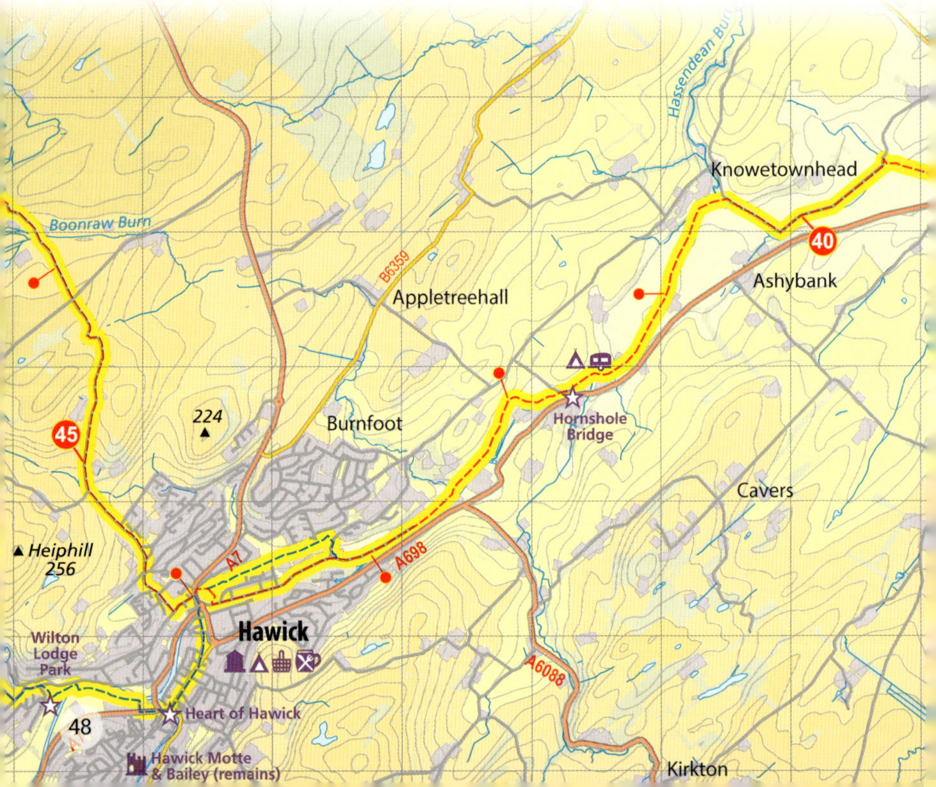

Rubers Law from Black Law

- Cross the stream and climb beside the plantation towards the mast of Black Law (338 m/1110 ft). At the top, turn left through a gate to head south-west for 100 m.
- Pass through two gates close together, then bear right (westward) across the open hillside. If visibility is poor, the waymarkers may not be intervisible: use map and compass.
- Follow the waymarkers as they lead you north-westerly across a small boardwalk, almost to the summit. Soon you reach the high point of this section of the Way at 320 m (1050 ft). The magnificent views include (to the west) the rocky summit of Rubers Law (424 m), a volcano last active some 330 million years ago. Bonchester Hill lies to the north-west.
- Descend steeply towards the Scots pines of Blacklaw Strip. After crossing the stile, continue beside the wood, and at its end turn left over the burn. Pass through various gates to reach a grassy path beside a drystone wall.

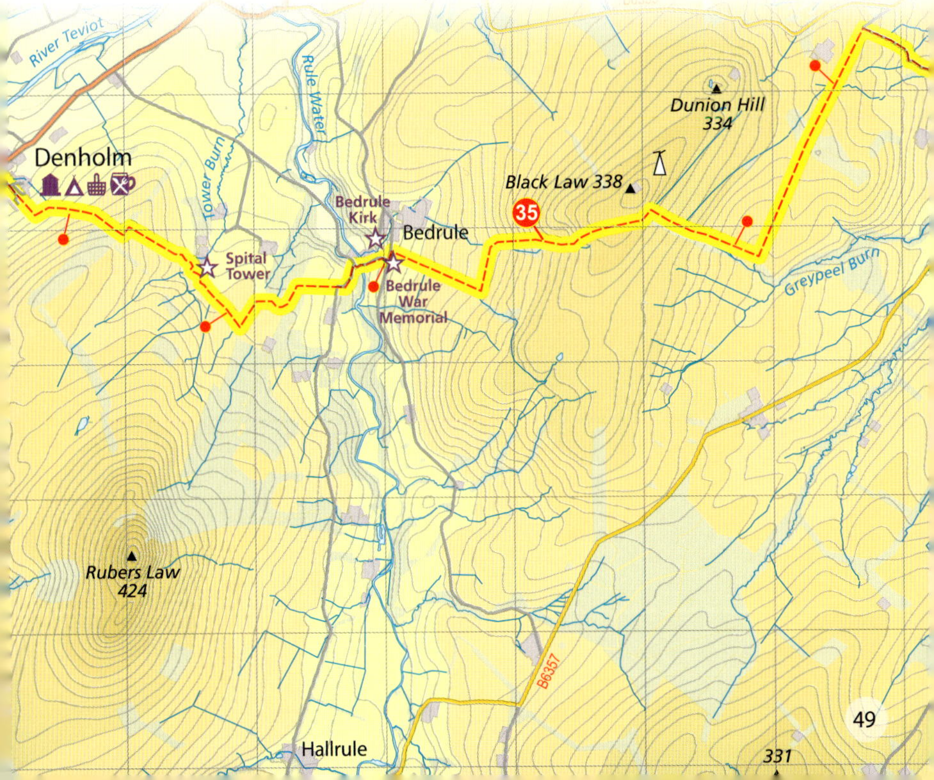

The Tower Burn, with Fatlips Castle on the skyline (circled)

- After 330 m of grassy path, exit by a gate and turn right onto the farm road. Continue downhill for 750 m to meet the minor road. The steeple of Bedrule Kirk is visible among the trees ahead.
- At the junction, turn left along the minor road for 70 m, and at the war memorial turn right on the road to Denholm. Cross the Rule Water by a stone bridge and follow the road around to the right.
- At a junction where a sign warns drivers about red squirrels, turn sharp left at the waymarker post. (If you are using OS sheet 331 dated 2015, ignore its incorrect route from this junction and for the next 2·8 km.) Follow the narrow road uphill towards Bonchester Bridge, around the S-bends to meet a track ahead.
- Continue up the farm track to enter a plantation. Turn left along the track to reach a gate and stile. Enter the field and bear right to follow the waymarkers through the gate into another field.
- Continue through the field with the plantation on your right towards a solitary tree. A waymarker post turns you left across the field to reach a ruinous stone wall. Continue beside the wall until you reach the second gate.
- To the right, you may see the 16th century peel tower, Fatlips Castle, on the rocky outcrop of Minto Crags. Its name recalls the over-familiar kissing with which ladies were greeted upon arrival.
- Cross into the next field and head towards the buildings, one of which is Spital Tower (sometimes spelled Spittal). Cross a burn and reach a farm track: turn right and continue through the gate next to the buildings of Ruberslaw Wildwood Camping (glamping also available: www.ruberslaw.co.uk).
- Turn left across a small stone bridge and continue uphill along the edge of the fields to reach a plantation.
- At the top of the hill, turn left beside the plantation, then after 80 m turn right through a gate and descend through the trees. Continue on the track known as The Loaning, which provides good views ahead to the Minto Hills and across the Teviot valley.

Memorial, Denholm village green

- Continue downhill on The Loaning and keep to it as it turns right and becomes a narrow tarmac road. Where this meets the A698 Jedburgh Road, bear left for 80 m along Eastgate to reach the heart of Denholm: see panel.
- To continue the Way, bear right along Kirkside, but to detour for Denholm's village green, pubs and bus stop, bear left instead.

> **Denholm**
>
> Denholm is a remarkable 17th century village planned around a huge village green used for grazing and for village fairs. The original village of 'Denum' was destroyed by English attacks in the 16th century. During the 18th century, with no bridge across the Teviot, it seems that most households owned a pair of stilts to cross the river. The memorial at the centre of the green is to Dr John Leyden (1775–1811), poet, antiquarian and linguist, and was erected in 1861. The green remains the focus of many village activities to this day, including games, rallies and the annual bonfire night.

- From Eastgate, bear right up the side of the village green (Kirkside), passing its 19th century parish church. Turn right into Leydens Road, and pass the restored thatched cottage that was John Leydon's birthplace
- Just after the garage, turn left along the B6405 road to follow it across the River Teviot, but immediately turn off left through the gate.
- Follow the banks of the river for 190 m through farmland and veer right, away from the river along the track. Continue along the track to meet the river again and keep following the banks until you reach steps.
- Climb the steps and follow the field boundary, which then descends to the road below. Turn left and follow the road running adjacent to the river for 1·5 km. At the waymarker, turn off the road just before Knowetown cottages.
- Continue through the trees, along the river and cross the wooden bridge over Hassendean Burn. Follow the path along this quiet stretch of river bank for 2 km to Hornshole Bridge.

Hornshole Bridge

- Hornshole Bridge crosses a tranquil section of the River Teviot, in contrast with its turbulent history. It was the site of a famous skirmish in 1514, which has a memorial on the south side of the bridge, as well as one in Hawick: see page 53.
- Keeping to the north side of the River Teviot follow the road for 70 m and turn left to rejoin the river bank. The riverside path continues and passes a weir. Opposite stands the Trow Mill, one of the original weaving mills serving Hawick's famous textile industry.
- Continue upstream for a further 1·2 km to a small parkland area on the outskirts of Hawick. Cross the Boonraw Burn and continue straight ahead following the river to meet the road.
- Follow Mansfield Road along the river past Hawick Rugby Football Club grounds to the roundabout.
- There's now a choice of routes: to keep to the Borders Abbey Way, continue along Mansfield Road for 1 km to approach the roundabout at Teviotdale Leisure Centre. The Way detours around the leisure centre to continue on Princes Street, but for the town centre, instead keep to the banks of the Teviot. Turn left to cross the river by the footbridge and head south on North Bridge Street. The town centre is about 350 m south of the bridge.

The alternative route into Hawick following the Waverley Walk is a more peaceful tree-lined approach that also avoids the heavy traffic that uses Mansfield Road.

From the rugby club roundabout, turn right into Hamilton Road and within 100 m turn off left onto a tarmac path.

After 60 m, turn left onto the Waverley Walk. This uses part of the old Waverley railway line and provides an attractive approach to the town parallel to the official Way. Continue past the town's cemetery for 1 km to reach Teviotdale Leisure Centre and rejoin the Way briefly.

To reach the town centre from the leisure centre, cross the A7 with care, but don't follow the Way into Princes Street. Instead head south on Dovemount Place and cross the Teviot by the footbridge and head south on North Bridge Street. The town centre is about 350 m south of the bridge.

East along the Teviot, Mansfield Road on the left

3·4 Hawick to Selkirk

Distance 12·8 miles 20·6 km
Terrain mainly farm and forest tracks, with some quiet roads
Grade long ascent from Hawick to Drinkstone Hill, then another long climb to Hartwoodmyres (summit of the Way at 338 m/1110 ft) with a total ascent of 430 m/1410 ft
Food & drink Hawick (wide choice), Selkirk (wide choice)
Summary interesting section starting on minor road, then climbing high with open vistas; some may prefer the longer drove road alternative, which follows a moorland ridge with wide views

Hawick (formerly *Hagawic*) refers to a settlement surrounded by hedging and likely dates back some 1500 years. Hawick was not associated with any abbey, however in the 12th century the Lovells, a Norman family associated with David I, were granted the lands.

They built a motte-and-bailey stronghold (Hawick Castle), but all that survives today is the motte (grassy mound). Nearby is Drumlanrig's Tower (now home to the Borders Textile Towerhouse). It was ruled by Baron Drumlanrig around 1412 and then by the Scott family or Dukes of Buccleuch around 1671.

Whilst Hawick derived income from town markets, the area was plagued by border conflicts. Cattle theft and looting was commonplace throughout the area. In 1514, the town's youths overpowered an English raiding party from Hexham at Hornshole, and captured their banner. The statue 'Ken the horse' depicts this post-Flodden success: see page 17. The victory is celebrated in Hawick every year as part of the Common Riding ceremonies.

In 1771, John Ballie introduced Hawick's first knitting loom and founded its long association with knitwear and Tweed cloth. The industry evolved to produce stockings and underwear, and then pullovers and cardigans. By the 19th century, the famous Tweed cloth was also being produced and collectively the industries supported the town. Even today, Hawick continues to produce some of these high quality products.

At the west end of the High Street a £10 million 'Heart of Hawick' regeneration project has three main elements: Tower Mill, a former spinning mill, has been transformed into a 108-seat cinema and theatre space and displays a 14-foot high Victorian waterwheel. It houses the Heritage Hub (a genealogy resource) and also includes the Borders Textile Towerhouse with VisitScotland iCentre: for more information, see page 68 and **www.hawickonline.com**.

'Ken the horse', Hawick High Street

Leaving Hawick, your choice is either to return to the Borders Abbeys Way or to continue through Hawick and join a drove road. The Way is shorter and better waymarked: see page 56. The historic drove road option, described below, rejoins the Way after 5·0 miles (8·1 km). Popular with equestrians joining from near Wiltonburn, this route adds 2·0 miles/3·3 km to your overall distance. Be prepared to follow directions closely through Hawick (no waymarkers) and on its offroad sections to find the terrain churned by horses' hooves. Its attractions are that it takes you through the centre of Hawick, it explores Wilton Lodge Park on the outskirts, and there are fine views from the ridge towards Drinkstone Hill.

Start from where North Bridge Street meets the north-east end of the High Street. The statue known as 'Ken the horse' ❶ was erected in 1914 to commemorate 400 years since the famous skirmish: see page 17. It soon became a local landmark, with a nickname from the local dialect: when asked for directions, residents would reply 'dive ee ken the horse? – gan past it ...' meaning 'do you know where the horse (monument) is? – go past it ...'.

Continue south-west along the High Street, passing the handsome town hall ❷ with clock tower designed by James Campbell Walker (1821-88). Soon after the town hall, you reach the 'Heart of Hawick' ❸: see page 53.

Bear right on the road to cross the Slitrig Water by Drumlanrig Bridge, and reach a roundabout where you bear left along Buccleuch Street. After 150 m, turn right along a lane at a blue 'Public Park' sign.

At the end of the lane turn left along the tarmac path past the River Teviot's weir, and onwards under the trees of Wilton Lodge Park: ❹ see panel.

Cross the arched bridge and turn left under the mature tree canopy, passing the shelter to arrive beside the fountain and the museum.

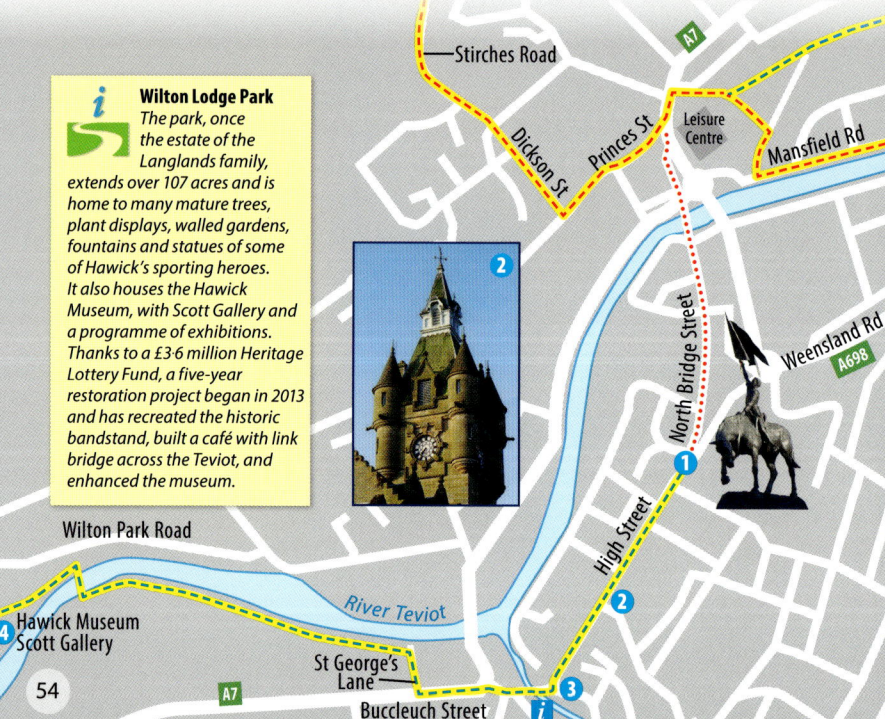

Wilton Lodge Park
The park, once the estate of the Langlands family, extends over 107 acres and is home to many mature trees, plant displays, walled gardens, fountains and statues of some of Hawick's sporting heroes. It also houses the Hawick Museum, with Scott Gallery and a programme of exhibitions. Thanks to a £3·6 million Heritage Lottery Fund, a five-year restoration project began in 2013 and has recreated the historic bandstand, built a café with link bridge across the Teviot, and enhanced the museum.

Continue past Hawick Museum and follow the route on the right towards the Scented Garden & Waterfall. Follow the stream up to the waterfall and climb the steps to exit the park onto Wilton Park Road.

Turn right and head straight uphill on Overhall Road. Turn left for 120 m, then turn right into Whitehaugh Road. Look behind you for fine views south over Hawick and beyond.

Follow this road, largely beside the Dean and Cala burns, uphill for 2·8 km. The tarmac then gives way to farm track at Calaburn Farm. Pass through the gates and turn right along the track.

After 150 m the track turns left and climbs alongside the plantation and past the farm building. Continue up the track past another plantation for 580 m to reach and go through a gate.

After the gate keep to the right-hand side, next to the coniferous plantation. At the top of the plantation, turn right through another gate for some great views: north-east to the Eildons, north-west to the Ettrick valley and Langhope Rig wind farm and south across Teviotdale to the hills beyond.

Cross the moorland on the faint track for 850 m along the ridge until you drop down to the right to a gate. Go through the gate and follow the well-defined track past Long Moss. Straight ahead is the cairn at the summit of Drinkstone Hill.

Continue south-east, and at the next waymarker descend past the dilapidated building to the gate.

Enter the field and descend between the two plantations. Upon reaching the stone wall, turn left and follow it to a metal gate. Go through the gate and turn left to rejoin the Borders Abbeys Way.

- To leave the centre of Hawick on the Borders Abbeys Way, head north up North Bridge Street and cross the pedestrian bridge. Continue on Dovemount Place for 120 m, then turn left up Princes Street. (Here you rejoin the Way which officially makes a loop around the Teviotdale Leisure Centre and crosses the A7).

- Turn right into Dickson Street and follow it uphill past Wilton Church where it becomes Stirches Road, which climbs steadily leaving Hawick behind. Beyond the derestriction sign it has no pavement or verges: be aware of oncoming traffic.

- You may notice the large building of St Andrews Convent on your right, seen through the parkland dotted with mature trees, and after about 900 m, Stirches Road passes its driveway.

- Keep straight on the road as it climbs through fields following the old stone dyke for 1·6 km past Stirches Mains Farm to a crossroads. From here, there are extensive views towards Rubers Law, Minto Hills, Liddesdale and the Cheviots.

- Go straight over the crossroads and keep on the road past Tandlaw farm, over Boonraw Burn and past Drinkstone farm. About 600 m after the crossroads, bear right just after a large shed.

- Continue for 300 m on gravel farm track and bear left at the next fork into the fields, keeping the wire fence on your left. The going underfoot is firm, stony in places.

East towards the Minto hills, with Cheviots distant at left

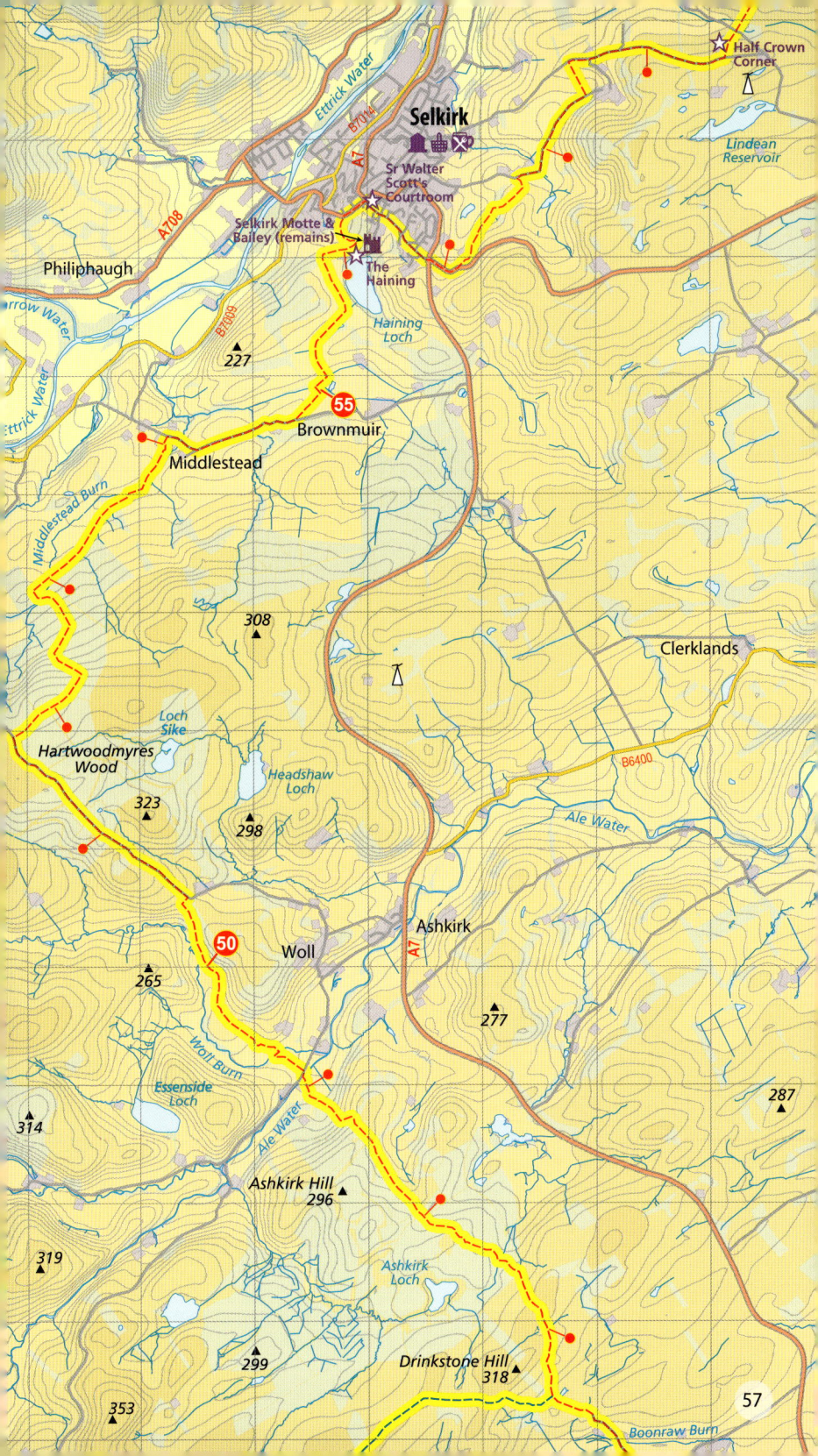

The drove road joins the Way from the left

- Enter the next field at a gate/stile, bearing right on a well-defined track across the pasture and uphill. You are joined by the Cross Borders Drove Road.
- Follow the track through the field and enter a further field. The track meanders in a northerly direction until it reaches a gate in a stone wall.
- Go through the gate and bear left through the forest glade, through another gate and down to cross the burn, the Falla Cleuch. Follow the track through the plantation, with the stone wall on your right, for 400 m to reach and go through a gate.
- Continue on the path through further forestry until you emerge on a well-defined track, and follow it.
- After 1 km on the track, at a junction go ahead on a narrow muddy path between a conifer plantation and a field. Emerge on a farm road and follow the waymarkers as they descend to pass between the house and outbuildings of Salenside Farm.
- Cross the Ale Water to meet the public road, where you turn right for just 50 m. Then turn left over the stile to follow an old right of way known as the Thief Road. Horse riders can follow alternative routes to avoid the golf course.
- ⚠ Follow the field boundary and enter the Woll Golf Course by the gate beside a ladder stile. Cross the golf course following the many waymarkers closely: they lead you for over 1·3 km across the Woll Burn, then beside a fine drystone wall. Please take great care when crossing fairways, be aware of flying golf balls and avoid distracting golfers whenever a ball is in play!

The Way beside the drystone wall

- Exit the golf course by the gate beside a ladder stile and climb on the farm track, with the Woll Burn meandering below to your left. Continue on the track through the forestry and out into a small field.
- Keep to the right of the field heading towards its north-west corner, adjacent to the wood. Cross over the stile onto a farm track. Turn right along the track to meet the public road at Wollrig.
- Turn left to follow the road for over 2 km as it heads towards the forestry in the distance, with views to the Cheviot hills behind. After 1·5 km you cross a cattle grid, and views open up to the north across the Yarrow Valley towards the Southern Uplands, with the distant Eildons on the right.

North towards the Eildons

- After a further 600 m, with clear felling to your right, a fingerpost turns you right onto a track into Hartwoodmyres Wood, with information board explaining the origin of its name and showing viewpoints.
- You soon reach the summit of the entire Way (338 m/1108 ft) on this track which provides fine views north-east to the Eildons, and, after the track veers left, towards the Ettrick valley.
- Continue on the track, following waymarkers that turn you successively right, then left and right again, descending through the remaining plantation and perhaps gaining your first glimpse of your destination, Selkirk, ahead.

Descending the plantation towards Selkirk

- Cross the Middlestead Burn and after 30 m leave the main track to join a grassy path bearing right alongside a wood. To the left there are fine views towards Bowhill Country House and Estate: see panel.
- Continue beside the wood to join a farm track through rough grasslands and descend to meet the Middlestead Burn again. Follow the track through the farmland beside the burn and pass through the steadings of Middlestead Farm in a left-right dogleg.
- At the junction with the public road, turn right and follow the quiet road for 1 km. The quiet road crosses Brownmoor burn and passes between fields.
- The road bends around the large sheds of Brownmoor. At the foot of the hill, turn left over the stile to enter a field. Head to the right edge, and pass around two sides of the field, then exit by a stile.

Bowhill

Bowhill is the ancestral home of the Dukes of Buccleuch, the hereditary Chief of the Scott clan. The land was once part of the vast Ettrick Forest and a royal hunting ground gifted to the clan by Robert the Bruce in 1322. According to legend, the name Buccleuch comes from a hunting incident where King Kenneth III was saved by John Scott, who wrestled a charging buck (male deer) to the ground in a deep cleuch or gorge. Bowhill House dates from 1708 and is home to a priceless art collection including works by Gainsborough, Reynolds and Canaletto. For visit information, see www.bowhillhouse.co.uk.

- After crossing the Hartwood Burn and another stile, turn right over a further stile to follow the field edges for 50 m, and meet a grassy farm track.
- Turn left onto the track to cross the field uphill and pass through a small wood. Follow the track as it bends right, then left, and soon The Haining will come into view.
- Through the trees, you may glimpse the Haining Loch. Keep to the track, passing a ruined dovecot near the end of the field and continue straight on through the wood.

Ruined dovecot

- Turn right onto a tree-lined driveway, passing stables, to join the main driveway to The Haining ❶, with the mansion house and loch to your right.
- The country house forms part of an estate originally owned by the Pringle family and dates back to the 1790s. In 2009 the house was bequeathed to the people of Selkirk, and its exhibition highlights the estate's history. For visit information, see **www.thehaining.co.uk**.
- Follow the driveway past the house and turn left leaving the estate under the gated arch at the public road, West Port. Cross the road and turn right to follow its pavement uphill for 240 m to arrive at Market Square, the centre of Selkirk.

Selkirk skyline

3.5 Selkirk to Melrose

Distance 10.5 miles 16.9 km
Terrain quiet roads, then farm and hill tracks followed by riverside paths
Grade gradual ascent from Selkirk rising up to Whitlaw Kips (285 m / 935 ft) followed by a long gradual descent to Melrose
Food & drink Selkirk (wide choice), Melrose (wide choice)
Summary lovely section across open hill on an old drove road offering surprisingly wide views, followed by a steady descent past Cauldshiels Loch and along the banks of the Tweed to return to Melrose

| Selkirk | 5.0 / 8.1 | Cauldshiels Loch | 2.5 / 4.0 | | 3.0 / 4.8 | Melrose |

Selkirk, meaning 'kirk of the forest' is one of the oldest settlements in the area and one of the oldest Royal Burghs in Scotland. Its townspeople are known as 'souters', meaning shoemakers or cobblers. The town lies in the heart of Borders country, above the Ettrick and Yarrow valleys.

Whilst no abbey remains in today's Selkirk, it was the site of the first abbey in the Scottish Borders, built by Tironensian monks in 1113. The structure was not made of stone, but probably from timber and thatch. The abbey's likely site was at Lindean Church to the north of the town. After 1128, upon the request of the monks, it was relocated to Kelso during the reign of King David I.

Selkirk once boasted its own motte-and-bailey castle, built in about 1119 but demolished in 1334. What little remains of the castle lies within The Haining Estate.

Selkirk's most famous citizen was Sir Walter Scott (1771-1832), Town Sheriff for over three decades. You can visit his Courtroom in Market Square. (The Way later passes his residence, Abbotsford House: see page 66.) Visit also Halliwell's House and Museum (admission free), which houses a VisitScotland Information Point: see page 68.

Selkirk's economy grew largely based on the wool trade, later with the production of tweed cloth. Many old mill buildings still stand by the Ettrick Water, once the basis of a bustling industry. Whilst production is much lower today, some mills still produce their famous cloths.

In 1867, Queen Victoria visited Abbotsford and enjoyed her tea with a slice of 'Selkirk Bannock'. The spongy, buttery raisin-filled bread was first commercially made by a local baker Robbie Douglas, and the Selkirk Bannock remains a popular local product to this day.

Sir Walter Scott's statue stands before his former Courtroom

Entrance to the Auld Kirk

- From Selkirk's Market Square, walk uphill past the 'Home of the Selkirk Bannock' into Kirk Wynd, passing the entrance to the Auld Kirk ('Kirk o' the Forest'). Its graveyard includes Commonwealth War Graves and the ancestors of President F D Roosevelt's mother are also buried here.

- Continue generally uphill on The Loan for 700 m to reach the main road (A7). Cross the A7 with care and continue ahead on the pavement of the road opposite. Pot Loch can be seen to the left below in the valley, as can the rolling hills on the horizon.

- After 280 m on a double-bend, leave the road by turning left onto a path which leads down into a woodland strip and into the golf course.

- Continue along the path, and at Caulk's Well bear left to follow the fine grassy path as it passes through heather, gorse and mixed trees.

- The path opens out into a wide grassy area crossed by many paths, but the Way heads straight on towards the red-roofed brick shelter. Take the steps at the rear of the building up into a wide valley, and follow waymarkers across the grassland.

Caulk's Well

- Turn left at a waymarker post and meet a lane at Buxton. Turn right along the narrow lane for 220 m, then bear left downhill on a farm track. Follow the track for 800 m, crossing a burn where an old stone bridge provides good views across Selkirk.

- Continue through a gate with fingerpost along the edge of the plantation, until a gate provides access into grazed fields and follow the old hedgerows.

- Just before Greenhead Farm, turn left through a gate and follow the waymarkers that take you around the field boundary and up to a high point. From here, a well-sited bench helps you to enjoy views across Selkirk, and to the Yarrow Valley beyond.

Following the undulating ridge

- Turn right to follow the channel-fenced approach to Shawmount. Follow the road uphill for 1 km to Halfcrown Corner, named because the Sunderland Estates paid the men who originally planted the woodland half a crown.
- Turn left opposite the huge radio mast, descending past buildings on the track through 'Woodlands' to meet another minor road.
- Cross the road and go straight ahead onto an old drove road that climbs past a plantation on the right. Follow the stone wall along the undulating ridge, which offers a wide panorama of the surrounding landscape.
- After passing through a gate, follow the wall for a further 1·3 km across the fields. As the wall veers right, the Eildons reappear on your right, and you descend to Faldonsidemoor.
- Continue north on the drove road as it rises past Dod Plantation on the left and descends to Cauldshiels Loch ahead on the right. Within 750 m of Faldonsidemoor, look out for the waymarker that turns you right, off the road to reach the loch. The loch is bounded by forest on the east and Cauldshiels Hill to the south, which sits upon an Iron Age fort.
- Local folklore has it that a water bull lives in the murky depths of this loch and lures the unsuspecting to a watery death. Upon visiting the loch, Washington Irving (an American novelist) wrote about his loch visit with Sir Walter Scott in his book *The Crayon Miscellany*.

Drove road descending to Cauldshiels Loch

- The Way skirts the northern shore of Cauldshiels Loch, then 100 m after leaving the drove road, it turns sharp left uphill at a waymarker, on a track. If the loch is very high, the path may be very muddy or even flooded: simply cut through the trees further back from the water, and turn left when you meet the track.

- Within 650 m of the loch, the track reaches a minor road where you turn right. Follow this road, with good views of the Eildons beyond the hawthorn hedge, and after 700 m turn left onto another minor road.

- This road twists and undulates, passing the lochan at Abbotsmoss and giving views ahead towards Tweedbank.

- After 800 m, you descend to a T-junction with another minor road. Turn left to follow this road as it winds downhill past a farm. About 500 m later, you reach and cross the B6360 to Abbotsford House ❶, a highly rated visit: see page 66.

Lochan at Abbotsmoss

Abbotsford House

Abbotsford House was built by the writer Sir Walter Scott (1771-1832) as a family home, and to display his valuable collection of books, artefacts and weaponry. His Waverley books were, for nearly a century, Europe's most popular novels. His study and library still have his writing desk and books exactly as he worked from them.

Reopened in 2013 after major refurbishment, the house and gardens welcome visitors from March to November (open 10.00-16.00, in season until 17.00). Admission charges apply: see www.scottsabbotsford.com.

Scott's library, with 7000 of his books

The Borders Abbeys Ways goes past Abbotsford's Visitor Centre, which is open year-round. Many walkers will appreciate its displays, restaurant and toilets, to which admission is free. From Abbotsford, it is only 1·2 miles/2 km to Tweedbank station.

Abbotsford House from the east

Bust of Scott in the library

- Leave Abbotsford with its Visitor Centre on your left, and follow a fingerpost pointing to Melrose (3 miles/5 km). Continue on the track towards the River Tweed. Veer right uphill and descend on a flight of steps to pass underneath the road at Galafoot Bridge.
- Keep to the path which soon leaves the riverside to pass through woodland. Briefly on tarmac, it passes the fringe of Tweedbank housing, then returns to the banks of the Tweed. Redbridge Viaduct lies ahead, 900 m beyond Galafoot Bridge.

Fingerpost pointing to the steps

- The viaduct carries the Borders Railway, and if Tweedbank station is your objective, leave the Way here by climbing the steps at a fingerpost. Turn right at the top to follow the trackside path which reaches the station after 730 m. (Don't be misled by the blue sign that claims it's only ¼ mile/400 m.)
- If your objective is to complete the Way to Melrose Abbey, you have a further 2·8 miles/4·5 km to walk. Continue under the viaduct and follow the riverside path as the Tweed veers right, to meet the main drive of Lowood House.
- Turn left, and at the end of the driveway, cross the main road to continue the riverside walk (shared with the Southern Upland Way). About 1·8 km after the viaduct, you pass the place where the outward route from Tweedbank station joined the Way at the B6374: see page page 27, second bullet.
- Beyond that, you pass the grounds of the Bay Waverley Castle Hotel and 1·8 km after the B6374 you reach the Mill Lade and the Chain Bridge.
- The Way continues on road past the bridge down to the junction with the B6361 where it turns right to reach Melrose Abbey within 900 m of the Chain Bridge. It ends at the abbey, where you may wish to celebrate your completion of the Borders Abbeys Way: congratulations!

Chain Bridge, Melrose

4 Reference

Useful websites and feedback on the route

The route is designated as one of Scotland's Great Trails, and maintained by Scottish Borders Council. Its page
   www.scotborders.gov.uk/bordersabbeysway
currently links to downloads of its 2007 booklet about the Way, but may be worth checking for updates. To offer feedback on the route, please contact the Ranger Service by phone 0300 100 1800 or email
   rangers@scotborders.gov.uk.

There's lots of information on the independently maintained site
   www.bordersabbeysway.com and on a range of websites listed on our page
   www.rucsacs.com/links/baw.

Historic Environment Scotland

This is the lead body that cares for Scotland's historic environment, including the Borders abbeys. Use its website to find out more:
   www.historicenvironment.scot.

Of the four abbeys on the Way, three charge for admission; only Kelso is generally free to enter during daylight hours (except winter Thursdays and Fridays).

Admission to the other three abbeys cost (in 2017) £6 for adults (16-59 years) or £4.80 (concessions), but if you have time to look at other HES properties such as Smailholm Tower and/or Hermitage Castle, then consider a Scottish Borders Explorer Pass which (in 2017) cost £28 (adults aged 16-59) or £14.40 (concession) and was valid for up to 30 consecutive days April-October.

Walking holiday packages

Walking Support was the first company to support the route in 2006 with the option of packages that include accommodation and baggage transfer: see
   www.walkingsupport.co.uk. Other companies are linked from our web page
   www.rucsacs.com/links/baw.

Transport and travel

For international journey planning, try
   www.rome2rio.com

Traveline journey planners cover travel between towns, cities, rail stations and airports throughout the UK:
   www.traveline.info

For rail travel in the UK or Scotland, you may prefer
   www.thetrainline.com or www.scotrail.co.uk.

For buses in the area, please refer to the map on page 10, which was correct when we went to press. For bus timetables, visit
   www.bustimes.org.uk or
   www.travelinescotland.com or the websites listed on page 10.

Visitor information and accommodation

VisitScotland is Scotland's official tourist organisation and its website
   www.visitscotland.com offers accommodation details and a booking service. It operates iCentres in Melrose (Priorwood Gift Shop), Kelso (inside the town hall), Jedburgh (beside the abbey), Hawick (Tower Mill, Heart of Hawick) and an Information Point in Selkirk (inside Halliwell's House Museum, April to October). Generally iCentres are open from 10.00 to 17.00, some open earlier and/or close later in season, and always with shorter hours on Sundays. Some are open in season only, and opening hours can change from year to year.

Email them at melrose@visitscotland.gov.uk, kelso@visitscotland.com, jedburgh@visitscotland.com, hawick@visitscotland.com and museums@scotborders.gov.uk. Apart from VisitScotland, there are specialist websites for B&B. For example,
   www.bedandbreakfastsearcher.co.uk
focuses on hotels and B&Bs, and lists them in order of distance from town centres.

For those who prefer a less conventional approach, consider also www.airbnb.co.uk.

Campsites

For campsites that accept tents, contact Melrose Gibson Park Caravan Club (01896 822 969, tents May-Sept only), Jedburgh Camping and Caravanning Club, Elliott Park, Jedburgh (01835 863 393), Ruberslaw Wildwood Camping, near Denholm (01450 870 092) and Riverside Caravan Park, Hornshole Bridge, near Hawick (01835 830 271).

The Scottish Outdoor Access Code

Scottish Natural Heritage is the government-funded body that works to care for Scotland's natural heritage, enabling people to enjoy it, helping people to understand and appreciate it, and supporting those who manage it:
   www.snh.org.uk

Details of the *Scottish Outdoor Access Code* (see page 12) are at
   www.outdooraccess-scotland.com.

The site has downloads for a pocket guide to the Code and also a *Dog Owners* leaflet. You can email SNH at enquiries@snh.gov.uk.

Further reading

Historic Scotland, now known as Historic Environment Scotland, has published official illustrated guides to Melrose Abbey, Jedburgh Abbey and Dryburgh Abbey. They are widely available in retail outlets in the Borders, and in the abbeys themselves.
In case of difficulty, the ISBNs are Melrose (978-1-90-357058-6), Jedburgh (978-1-84917-022-2) and Dryburgh (978-1-84917-072-7).

Turnbull, Ronald (2012) *Battle Valleys: a portrait of the Border* Frances Lincoln 978-0-7112-3229-7

This beautiul hardback has great photographs, well-informed and readable text and gives the reader a whole new perspective on the Borders: highly recommended.

Maps: printed and online

Ordnance Survey marks the Way with green lozenges in its Explorer series (1:25,000) on sheets 331, 338, 339 and OL16. OS maps are widely available in retail outlets and online, e.g.
   www.aboveandbeyond.co.uk.

Please visit our online route map at
   www.rucsacs.com/routemap/baw and zoom in for amazing detail on the route and its points of interest: see inside back cover for a screen clip.

Weather forecast

The Met Office is the authoritative source for weather information in Britain. Visit their websites:
   www.metoffice.gov.uk and
   www.metoffice.gov.uk/mobile

The BBC's five-day and ten-day forecasts are available from www.bbc.co.uk/weather – search for Melrose, Kelso, Jedburgh, Hawick or Selkirk.

Notes for novices

For those who are new to long-distance walking, our website offers *Notes for novices* with suggestions on choosing and using gear, including boots, rucksack, gaiters, poles, water carrier and blister treatment. Find them at www.rucsacs.com.

Acknowledgements

The author and publisher wish to thank the Beeslack, Penicuik Camera Club (Audio Visual Group) for its members' generous provision of photographs, and its Chairman John Barnett for organising access. They also thank Susan Gray of Scottish Borders Council and John Henderson of Walking Support for many valuable comments on the draft manuscript.

Photo credits

John Barker p17u, pp28-29, p34l, pp46-47, p51, p62; **John Barnett** p28u; **G Cattermole** p16; **Rob Gray** p17l; **Lynne Kirton** p20u, p21u, p21l, p25 (inset), p26l; **Herbert Kratky**/istockphoto.com p20m; **Neil Mackay** pp30-31; **Danny McClure** p36, p51l; **Jacquetta Megarry** pp6-7, p8 (all), p9 (all), pp26-27, p27u, p29 u and inset, p32, p33u, p38 (both), p45 (both), p46u, p47u, pp51/52, p53, p54, p56 (all), p58l, p59 (both), p61 (both), p63l, p64u, p65, p66 (u and m), p67u; **Brian Salvona** pp4-5, p12, p18 (u and m), pp20-21, p25l, p35 (both), p40 (both), p42, p43 (both), p48, p49, p50, p52, p58u, p60, p63u, p64l; **Gordon Simm** p24l, p26u; p15 **Wikimedia**.

The following images are licensed from **Dreamstime.com** jointly with the respective photographers: p11 **Petr Švec**; p15 **Ivan Kravtsov**; pp18/19; **Julianelliott**; 21u (inset) **Joan Egert**; p21m **Martin Pelanek**; pp18/19 **Julianelliott**; p22u **Davemhuntphotography;** p22l **Mikelane45**; p23u **Steve Allen**; p23l **Elena Duvernay**; p24u, p25u **12qwerty**; p33l **Steve Morris**; p34u, p37 **Creativehearts**; p39u **Sue120502**; p39l **Gail Johnson;** p66l **Juliane Jacobs**; p67l **Aidant**.

69

Index

A
4 Abbeys Cycle Route 13
Abbotsford House 11, 62, 65, 66
accommodation 11, 68

B
bus services 10, 27, 68
butterflies 20, 21

C
camping 11, 14, 68
Common Ridings 13, 17, 53
cycling 13

D
Denholm 10, 11, 51, 68
dipper 22
dogs 12
drove roads 5, 7, 9, 54, 58, 64
Dryburgh Abbey 7, 15, 34, 68, 69

F
farmland 20-21, 26
Floors Castle 37
fox 24

G
geology and scenery 18-19
goosander 23
gradients 8, inside back cover
grouse, red 26

H
habitats and wildlife 20-26
harebell 25
hare, brown 20
Hartwoodmyres Wood 59
Hawick 4, 5, 7, 10, 11, 14, 17, 52-56, 68
heather 26
heron, grey 23
Hornshole Bridge 11, 17, 51, 52, 53, 68
history 15-17

J
Jedburgh 4, 5, 7, 10, 11, 13, 14, 17, 45, 47, 68
Jedburgh Abbey 15, 43, 46, 68, 69
Jedburgh Castle Jail and Museum 45, 47

K
Kelso 4, 5, 7, 10, 11, 14, 15, 36, 37, 38, 40, 62, 68
Kelso Abbey 15, 39, 68, 69
King David I 4, 15, 16, 28, 39, 46, 62

M
Melrose 4, 5, 7, 10, 11, 14, 15, 27, 28, 29-31, 67, 68
Melrose Abbey 15, 28, 29, 68, 69

O
orchid, common spotted 26
otter 22

P
packing checklist 14

R
reivers 16, 17
rivers and riverbanks 22-23
River Teviot 4, 18, 22, 38, 40, 42, 45, 49, 51, 52, 54
River Tweed 18, 27, 28, 35, 67
roe deer 24

S
Scott, Sir Walter 34, 45, 62, 64, 66
Scottish Outdoor Access Code (SOAC) 12, 69
Selkirk 62
skylark 21
Smailholm Tower 19, 36, 68
squirrels, red and grey 24-25

T
Temple of the Muses 4, 33
terrain 8
Thomson, James 4, 33
transport and travel 10, 68
Tweedbank 10, 27, 66, 67

W
Waverley Walk 9, 52
waymarking and navigation 9
weather 6, 8, 69
wildlife 20-26
William Wallace statue 33
woodland and forestry 24-25
wren 21

Y
yellowhammer 21